Judaic Spiritual Psychotherapy

Aaron Rabinowitz

UNIVERSITY PRESS OF AMERICA,® INC.
Lanham • Boulder • New York • Toronto • Plymouth, UK

Copyright © 2010 by
University Press of America,® Inc.
4501 Forbes Boulevard
Suite 200
Lanham, Maryland 20706
UPA Acquisitions Department (301) 459-3366

Estover Road
Plymouth PL6 7PY
United Kingdom

All rights reserved
Printed in the United States of America
British Library Cataloging in Publication Information Available

Library of Congress Control Number: 2010927695
ISBN: 978-0-7618-5183-7 (paperback : alk. paper)
eISBN: 978-0-7618-5184-4

∞™ The paper used in this publication meets the minimum
requirements of American National Standard for Information
Sciences—Permanence of Paper for Printed Library Materials,
ANSI Z39.48-1992

Contents

1	Introduction and Brief History	1
2	Judaic Psychotherapy	9
3	Principles of Judaic Spiritual Psychotherapy	25
4	Methodology	39
5	Meditation: The Judaic View	48
6	Forgiveness: Critique of the "Sunflower"	59
7	Conclusion: Values in Psychotherapy	74

Chapter One

Introduction and Brief History

The closing years of the 20th century witnessed a rapprochement between psychology and religion. This parallels a similar trend, both in the general population and in the sciences. Whereas in the 19th and early 20th centuries, religion and spirituality were denigrated by many, this trend has stopped. On the contrary, their role, especially that of spirituality, has gained respect and influence. As for psychology, much research on religion and spirituality has been recorded in scientific articles and books have been published by mainstream publishers, including the American Psychological Association. Hundreds of articles chronicling the research on the relation between mental health and religion have appeared in respectable psychological and medical journals. The American Psychological Association has a section of professionals specializing in the interface between religion and psychology.

Initially, therapy was viewed as an intrapersonal process revolving around drives and instincts. With the passage of time, it was broadened to include interpersonal and cultural factors. New therapeutic approaches emerged. Even psychoanalytic theory and its techniques were recast to include these factors. Humanistic psychology insisted that values were crucial for understanding personality. All these contributed to changes in the psychotherapeutic process. Ego-psychology, object relations theory, and Kohut's self-psychology are outgrowths of these developments creating a broader, less rigid picture of personality, psychopathology, and psychotherapy.

The changing scientific philosophical understanding of the exact sciences, especially in physics, is also a cardinal factor in fully comprehending the emergence of therapeutic spiritual psychotherapy and its acceptance into mainstream psychology. In its formative years, psychology and psychotherapy aspired to be recognized as a branch of science. It, therefore, had to conform to the then accepted criteria defining science; meaning it is not to be shaped by values or hampered by philosophical speculations. However, the very nature of science has undergone a metamorphosis. Scientists no longer visualize an orderly Newtonian universe governed by clear-cut laws. Relativity theory, quantum physics, Heisenberg's uncertainty principle, and Bohr's complementarity principle have altered the way physicists perceive the world. More recently, Bell's theorem, the experiments of Alain Aspect and others confirming the non-locality principle have changed the face of science. Wheeler, a major prominent physicist, claims that our universe is an observer-created universe; the past has no existence until it is recorded in the present. Wigner singles out consciousness as the factor which bestows meaning to quantum results. Many scientists and philosophers of science see in the new physics a close affinity to mysticism.[1] Such assertions by world-renowned physicists paved the way for a more congenial perception of spirituality and religion. The development of therapeutic spiritual psychotherapy mirrors the continuous expansion of the horizons of science. Psychology can now allow itself to break the narrow confines it imposed upon itself in the past. It can now include values, ideals, spirituality, and religion as legitimate concerns of psychology and psychotherapy.

Richards and Bergen[2] record the attitudes and beliefs of the founders of psychology and trace the change in those attitudes. They write:

"Although it was not always done explicitly or even deliberately, the early leaders of the psychoanalytic and behavioral theories, and other early leaders in experimental psychology . . . as was true of other scientists," believed that, "human behavior could be explained naturalistically without resorting to spiritual and transcendent explanations. . . . Perhaps because of their personal beliefs about religion and perhaps because science in the late nineteenth and early 20th centuries were vigorously challenging religious authority and tradition, psychoanalysis and behavioral theories were not only naturalistic, but also portrayed religious beliefs and behaviors in negative ways. For example, in the *Future of an Illusion*, Freud stated that religious ideas are "illusions, fulfillments of the oldest, strongest and most urgent wishes of mankind." He also stated that religion is the "universal obsessional neurosis of humanity." They note that both Freud and Watson rejected the religious faiths of their parents and replaced those beliefs with their own naturalistic, atheistic psychological faith. Other psychological greats are also cited as having rejected their faith, such as Skinner, Hall, Wolpe, Bandura, and Rogers. Philip Rieff, the astute thinker and analyst of Freud's thinking and development, writes that of the topics discussed by Freud, it is on the topic of religion that his analytic reasoning faculties failed him.[3]

One cannot overemphasize the influence of Darwinism on Freud and other psychologists. I have discussed this elsewhere[4] quoting Ellenberger who wrote, "the most important influence of Darwinism was felt through Social Darwinism, that is, the indiscriminate application of the concepts of "struggle for life," "survival of the fittest," and "elimination of the unfit," to the facts and problems of human societies. He supports his opinion by citing a list of injustices perpetrated in the name of Social Darwinism; for example: "Militarists throughout the world turned it into a scientific argument for the necessity of war and for maintaining armies. . . A long series of politicians proclaimed the same principle, culminating with Hitler who repeatedly invoked Darwin."

The unconscious of Freudian theory, predicated on biology and drawing from Darwinism, inevitably leads to its perception as a repository of hedonistic and aggressive instincts. I attempt to show in my book (see note 3) that Rabbi Israel Salanter's concept of "inner forces" is similar to the Freudian unconscious, only in that it has the dynamic characteristics that the unconscious has. The characteristics of the unconscious which stem from its being conceived in a biological framework are conspicuously absent from the inner forces of Salanterian theory. As will be demonstrated further on, the position of the author is that the concept of the unconscious can serve to help explain behavior and to deepen our understanding of scripture and the teachings of the sages.

There are, of course, other factors which influenced and shaped the antireligious attitude of many early psychologists. The assumptions of positivism and empiricism were very instrumental in their mode of thinking. Perusal of this issue can be profitable and the reader is referred to Richards and Bergin, note 2, and to my book, note 3. There were, of course, some who did not succumb entirely to their accepted mode of thinking. Mention should be made of Allport, the humanistic and existential schools of psychology, as well as Jung, and even some Freudian psychologists.

As previously noted, discoveries in physics which slowly, but surely brought about changes in the philosophy of science, and the emerging fields of research in brain functioning and consciousness, helped to alter the zeitgeist. Determinism and reductionism, the mainstays of psychology, began to crumble and consequently opened the door to religion and even more so to spirituality. Another important cog operative in this change is the research on mental health and religion. Whereas it was once commonly held that religion has a deleterious effect on mental health, new research has completely altered the picture. The findings provide evidence that religious beliefs are positively related to many indicators of emotional and social adjustment. Many therapists now believe that such beliefs and behaviors are resources for promoting therapeutic change.[5] The boundaries which existed between the different therapeutic approaches are now much more flexible and permissive of integration. This paves the way for spiritual therapeutic techniques to also become an integral part of the therapist's methodology. Finally, the reemergence of values as a legitimate part of psychology promotes the use of spiritual psychotherapy. David Campbell, in his presidential address in 1975 to the American Psychological Association, said: "A major thesis of this address is that present-day psychology and psychiatry in all their major forms are more hostile to the inhibitory messages of traditional religious moralizing than is scientifically justified . . . psychology and psychiatry . . . not only describe man as selfishly motivated, but implicitly teach that he ought to be so."

RELIGION-SPIRITUALITY

Up to this point, the terms *spirituality* and *religion* have been used interchangeably as if they are synonyms. In truth, there are important differences between them, denoting differing aspects of the human psyche and personality. Miller[6] writes: "For as long as history has been recorded, humankind has assumed that reality is not limited to the material sensory world. . . Whatever behavioral scientists and health care professionals may themselves believe, the spiritual side of human nature remains important to many or most clients. A substantial minority at least describe spirituality as the most important source of strength and direction in their lives. Many prominent voices in the history of psychology have raised spirituality as a proper subject for scientific study. Like personality and health, spirituality is complex. . . However defined, whether broadly as consciousness, or in relation to transcendence, spirituality (like personality or character) is an attribute of individuals. Religion, in contrast, is an organized social entity. . . Differences clearly exist, however, with religious factors focused more on prescribed beliefs, rituals, and practices as well as social instinctual factors. Spiritual factors, on the other hand, are concerned more with individual, subjective experiences, sometimes shared with others . . . . Spirituality can then be defined apart from religion, and the relationships between the two become a matter for empirical study. Before leaving this point, though, it is worthwhile to note that this sharp distinction between spirituality and religion that some currently make has not always been emphasized. When William James wrote *The Varieties of Religious Experience* a century ago, he was clearly describing the boarder domain that is now called spirituality.

This book presents my perception of Judaic Spiritual Psychotherapy. It adopts James' view and, from a Judaic perspective, does not distinguish between religion and spirituality which radiate a subjective aura. Judaism is wary of spiritual subjectivism. The emphasis on subjectivity is rooted in the sagacious conception of religion by Friedrich Schliermacher, a German philosopher and student of religion in the late 18th and early 19th centuries. He perceived religion as a religious experience which he felt enabled him to refute Kant's critique of religion. Kant, himself, in line with his critical analysis, understood religion primarily as espousing morality. Schliermacher saw it as an emotional experience. He evolved this so as to create what he deemed an impregnable fortress for religion, safe from scientific onslaught, safe from the constant changes in understanding what constitutes truth. For him, the "religious experience" is the crux and essence of religion. In essence, he attempted to cast religion as an autonomous movement that cannot be reduced to metaphysics, science, or morality, but rather insists on the primacy of affect, on feeling and emotion. These emphases, which are intrinsically coupled with subjectivity and entail a neglect of norms, are foreign to Judaism.

Rabbi Dr. Soloveitchik views with great trepidation the position which tends "to deliver philosophical thinking from the yoke of reason" and sees it as one of the causes of the unleashing of the dark forces of this century (the 20th century).[7] He writes: "When reason surrenders its supremacy to dark, equivocal emotions, no dam is able to stem the rising tide of the affective stream. . . Indeed, it is of greater urgency for religion to cultivate objectivity than perhaps for any other branch of human culture." Rabbi Soloveitchick is sympathetic to the concept of the direct religious experience, but anchors it to objectivity and norms—Halacha.[8] Tillich, the eminent Christian theologian, is also strongly critical of extreme subjectivity. He, as well, points to the potential for destructiveness inherent in this approach.[9]

THEISTIC SPIRITUAL PSYCHOTHERAPY

What follows is a short and hopefully concise description of the main tenets of spiritual psychotherapy. I confine myself to Richards and Bergin's approach which they feel can be incorporated into mainstream psychotherapeutic tradition.[10]

The core assumptions are that God exists and that humans are His creation and that there is a link between God and humans. Humans can communicate with Him through prayer and various spiritual practices. God has revealed moral truths to guide humans and the human spirit or soul continues to exist after death. The philosophical underlying assumptions are in conflict with the deterministic, reductionistic, mechanistic, relativistic, and hedonistic principles assumed by many scientists. As has been discussed earlier in this chapter, they note that contemporary post-modern views in science and philosophy are now more compatible with this theistic perspective than in the past.

They posit that the spirit or soul "interacts with other aspects of the person to produce what is normally referred to as personality and behavior." The core essence of identity and personality is spiritual. "People who believe in their eternal spiritual identity follow the influence of God's spirit and live in harmony with universal moral principles are more likely to develop in a healthy manner socially and psychologically. Therapeutic change can be facilitated through psychological, social, educational and spiritual interventions. They, however, believe that "complete healing and change require a spiritual process. Therapeutic change is facilitated, and is more often profound and lasting, when people heal and grow spiritually through God's inspiration in their lives. Spiritual practices such as prayer, meditation, readings, sacred writings, worship and ritual, repentance and forgiveness, altruistic service, and seeking spiritual direction can give people added hope and power to cope, heal, and change."

Richards and Bergin emphasize that their approach does not advocate that the therapist should somehow tend to influence the client to adopt the therapist's values. Moreover, even if the client's values are akin to those of the therapist, it does not follow that the therapy should include specific instructions as how to apply set values in their lives. Therapists must allow clients to make their own choices, both as to values and their application. On the other hand, this does not negate what they feel is the therapist's responsibility to share "what wisdom they can about values when it is relevant to the client's problems."

A body of spiritual interventions is recommended which can be used by psychologists. These include "praying for clients, encouraging clients to pray, discussing theological concepts, making reference to scriptures, using spiritual relaxation and imagery techniques, encouraging repentance and forgiveness, helping clients live congruently with their spiritual values, self-disclosing spiritual beliefs or experiences, consulting with religious leaders, and recommending religious bibliotherapy." This extensive list does not exhaust all the interventions mentioned in the literature; for example, meditative techniques and acceptance.

Other issues are also discussed by Richards and Bergin, insofar as they are related to theistic spiritual psychotherapy: the need to establish a spiritually open and safe relationship. They note that spiritual beliefs are often private and sacred to people. Much care and sensitivity has to be shown in the therapeutic relationship to respect those feelings. To cite one example: "Differences in religious affiliation and disagreements about specific religious doctrines or moral behaviors can threaten the therapeutic alliance if they are prematurely disclosed or inappropriately addressed. The authors relate to a number of issues. I think it is appropriate in closing this section to mention an additional issue they discuss which I feel is relevant to Judaic spiritual psychotherapy. They write: "Psychotherapists who implement a spiritual perspective in their professional practices are faced with several potentially difficult ethical questions and challenges. Dual relationships (religious and professional), displacing or usurping religious authority, imposing religious values on clients, violating work-setting (church-state) boundaries, and practicing outside of the boundaries of professional competence are all potential ethical pitfalls."

The use of spiritual intervention in conjunction with psychological psychotherapy is contraindicated (they feel) where: (a) "clients have made it clear when they do not wish to participate in such interventions; (b) when clients are delusional or psychotic; (c) when spiritual issues are clearly not relevant to clients presenting problems; (d) when clients are minors and their parents have not given the therapist permission to use spiritual interventions; and (e) when therapy takes place in a public, tax-supported setting that requires exclusion of religious concerns."

This presentation of Richards and Bergin's approach is not meant to cover it in its entirety. It does not, of course, relate to other approaches, but it serves, I believe, as an adequate introduction to the topic. My understanding of the principles and methods of Judaic Spiritual Psychotherapy follows. I trust it will be apparent to the reader where and how the Judaic approach differs in some of its principles and methodology.

NOTES

1. Barbour, Ian (1990). Religion in an Age of Science. San Francisco: Harper & Row. P. 115.

2. P. Scott Richards & Allen E. Bergin (1997). A Spiritual Strategy for Counseling and Psychotherapy. Washington, DC: American Psychological Association, Chapters 2 and 3.

3. Rieff, P. (1970). Freud: The Mind of the Moralist, 3d ed. Chicago: The University of Chicago Press. P. 257. Quoted in my book Judaism and Psychology: Meeting Points. New Jersey/Jerusalem: Jason Aronson, Inc. See Chapter 2 for further discussion of this issue.

4. See note 3, in my book, PP. 69-74.

5. Richards & Bergin, note 2, quote extensive research on P. 42.

6. Integrating Spirituality into Treatment. Miller, William R. Ed. (1999). Washington, DC: American Psychological Association. PP. 5-7.

7. Soloveitchick, Joseph B. (1983). Halakhic Man. Philadelphia: Jewish Publication Society of America. Notes to Part 1, no. 4. See also The Halakhic Mind (1986). PP. 53-55. New York: The Free Press. The latter quotation is from there.

8. Soloveitchick, Joseph B. (1979). Ubikasthem Meshom. Ish Halakah-Golu Venistar. Jerusalem: Histadrut Tziyonit Olamit. PP. 128-129. Prof. Waxman, Professor of Sociology and Jewish Studies at Rutgers University, distinguishes between two types of spirituality. "I'm not speaking of a spirituality that is personalistic or individualistic through which people try to find what's meaningful for themselves. That does not involve any commitments. I am talking about a spirituality that has significance to one's life to the extent that it involves commitment—to tradition, to institutions, and to the group." Quoted in YU Review, Fall, 2005, Yeshiva University, New York, P. 10.

9. Tillich, Paul (1952). The Courage to Be. New York/New Haven/London: Yale University Press. PP. 148-149.

10. Casebook for a Spiritual Strategy in Counseling and Psychotherapy. Ed. P. Scott Richards and Allen E. Bergin (2004). Washington, DC: American Psychological Association. See Chapter 1.

Chapter Two

Judaic Psychotherapy

Proper understanding of Judaic Spiritual Psychotherapy requires that, firstly, the relation of psychotherapy, in general, to Judaic thought be explored and analyzed. I have discussed this issue in previous writings.[1] This chapter summarizes some of that material and expands upon it.

A basic question is whether biblical and rabbinic concepts can be viewed as being a basis for anchoring psychotherapy to Jewish thought. If, indeed, there are such concepts, what are they and how are they to be understood? These issues have been addressed and various analyses and approaches have been proposed. My feeling is that psychotherapy is best perceived from a Judaic standpoint as a healing and, in a certain sense, an educative process.[2] I posit that this is even more so for psychotherapy which integrates into its philosophy and methodology spiritual values, irrespective of what this unique psychotherapy is called. This last sentence is added so as to make it clear that this new psychotherapy is called by a number of different names in the literature. These range from spiritual psychotherapy to theistic psychotherapy, integrative spiritually oriented psychotherapy, humanistic integrative spiritual psychotherapy, or, as some prefer, spiritual counseling.

Miller[3] calls attention to the fact that the history of psychotherapy is not the story of the insane or their treatment. He quotes Shafranske, a pioneer in the field of spiritual psychotherapy, who writes that psychotherapy is a young science which originated with Sigmund Freud and the discovery of the unconscious. Psychotherapy is defined as the method which has as it goal "the alleviation of mental and emotional distress that may have biological referents, but the source of which are thought to be in some way in a person's relationships, past or present with other persons, which relationship in some way changes the style, if not the nature, of other relationships." It is noteworthy that, notwithstanding the premise that psychotherapy is not the treatment of the insane, which is predicated upon a healing process, psychotherapy can be characterized as a healing progression. Changing the nature of a person's relationships with others is a healing, educative undertaking. Some therapies attempt to effect this change through elucidation and interpretation; other therapies include feeling and affect as an integral part of the above or even as the main part, that which causes the change. Others advocate cognitive restructuring, and yet others stress behavior change as the sought after goal and the fulcrum effecting the change. The above is only a partial list of therapies practiced today. Not only do they differ in their basic orientation which, in turn, is rooted in differing philosophies of the perception of human nature, but a wide divergence exists as to the methodologies employed.

Jerome Frank[4] has defined the components of psychotherapy as having (a) a socially sanctioned healer; (b) a sufferer who seeks relief; and (c) a program designed to offer relief. Miller, mentioned above, writes: " . . . both modern spiritualities and modern psychotherapies opt for integration, seeing the fullness of human nature being as comprising the physical, the mental, the emotional, and the spiritual." Miller goes on to document the role of healers from ancient times to the present, emphasizing in particular the paths of spirituality and psychotherapy.

This description of the nature and function of psychotherapy lends itself easily to the addition of spirituality as a factor in psychotherapy. Its importance for many clients, the emotional impact it carries, and the influence it may have previously exerted on the client qualify it to be an integral and important part of the process of psychotherapy.

THE JEWISH BASIS FOR VIEWING PSYCHOTHERAPY AS HEALING

Jewish therapists have proposed a number of concepts which underlie and constitute the basis for a psychotherapy rooted in Judaic thought. Some see "arevut"—the Hebrew word signifying mutual responsibility, as the Jewish bedrock of therapy. Others propose that "hocheach tochiach"—the obligation to reprove others for their misdeeds, as the concept which best serves as the Judaic basis of psychotherapy. Others regard "vidu"—confession, as grasping the essence of Judaic-rooted psychotherapy. I've discussed this issue in my book (note no. 1, in chapter 6). There I expressed my astonishment that the concepts of education and reeducation were not mentioned by Jewish psychotherapists. Historically, Oskar Pfister, a Protestant pastor who was Freud's friend, saw in education the basis of psychotherapy. I feel that the healing-educative model best expresses the Judaic approach. Let's consider healing; it is associated with malfunctioning, attending to the physically sick. Surprisingly, nowhere does the Bible invoke a specific commandment to do so. This omission is rather startling and bears explaining. The sages explain that the performance of good deeds, "chesed"—loving-kindness—is subsumed under the injunction to walk in God's ways:

"For if ye shall diligently keep all these commandments which I command you, to do it, to love the Lord your God, to walk in all His ways, and to cleave unto Him." (Deuteronomy 11:22)

"After the Lord God shall ye walk, and Him shall ye fear, and His commandments shall ye keep, and unto His voice shall ye hearken, and Him shall ye serve, and unto Him shall ye cleave." (Deuteronomy 13:15)

The sages interpret walking in His ways to mean adopting His traits (Talmud Bavli, Sotah 14:A). He clothes the naked, therefore we should clothe them; in like fashion as He visits the sick, comforts the bereaved, and buries the dead, so we humans should perform these deeds. This interpretive clarification is quoted by Rashi, the greatest medieval Jewish commentator on the Torah, adding (Deuteronomy, 13:5) that the injunction to perform "chesed"—acts of loving-kindness—is ordained by the phrase and "unto Him shall ye cleave." This places these actions on the most lofty, spiritual plane to which a human can aspire—to cleave unto the Almighty.

The above Talmudic passage listing acts of "chesed" does not include healing the sick and, as previously noted, this intriguing omission calls for an explanation. Nahaminides [Ramban] in his biblical commentary [Leviticus, 26:11] writes that the divine promise that He will reside among Israel means that the Israelites will be healthy and will not require a physician's services. He quotes:

"I will put none of the diseases upon thee, which I have put on the Egyptians for I am the Lord that healeth thee." (Exodus, 15:26)

Nahaminides explains that during the prophetic era, a righteous sick person would not seek a physician's services, but would turn to the prophet to ascertain the spiritual cause of the illness. Assa, king of Judea, is reprimanded because he sought medical assistance when he took sick (Chronicles 2, 16:1). According to Nahaminides, the verse in Exodus, 2:19 "and shall cause him to be thoroughly healed" permits the physician to minister to the patient and entitles him to reimbursement. The physician should not refrain from doing so on the pretext that illness is God's punishment and, therefore, only He can heal. However, a righteous person during the prophetic era was obligated to turn to the prophet, not to a physician. To avert misunderstanding, after the destruction of the first temple at which time prophecy ceased, it became common practice to seek medical aid. Nahaminides himself was a physician. Following this train of thought, we can now understand why healing the sick is not included in the Talmudic list of acts of "chesed" being that during the prophetic era, a God-fearing person would not turn to a physician. This may sound strange since there are only a limited number of prophets whose prophecies are recorded and who, therefore, are known to us. The Talmud teaches that, in actuality, there were very many prophets, but only those whose prophecies are relevant for all time were recorded and included in the complete Bible. In our time, there is no question but that a therapist who alleviates the emotional psychic pain of another individual is walking in the ways of the Almighty. This is so for any therapy which can lighten the burden of suffering. How much more so is this true for psychotherapists who, under certain conditions, deem it necessary to integrate spirituality into the fabric of the therapeutic process.[5]

Knight,[6] a minister and psychiatrist, traces psychotherapy to specifically Christian roots. He believes that healing includes a "quality of mastery—the gift of healing." He ties it to charismatic authority. The model proposed by him can lead to a blurring of important distinctions and differences between the functions of religion and psychotherapy. Casting religion in the role of healer can lead one to falsely believe that religion's primary function is healing. He writes, "The emphasis all along has been more on the technological challenges of treating disease than on the consideration of the religious, psychological, and social dimensions of illness and patienthood . . . Much needs to be done to convince students of the healing arts that the outcome of their interventions with patients may depend less on their technical skills than on the quality of their relationships with patients, and their knowledge of the patients' life situation . . . Relevant to this task is the counsel of the renowned physician, Sir William Osler. It is more important to know what sort of patient has a disease than what sort of disease a patient has."

The two scholarly chapters (note 6) contain many valuable insights and fascinating interpretations of the role of healer. He buttresses his ideas with quotes from Scripture, mythology, and leading theologians and physicians. However, investing the healer, whether a surgeon or a psychiatrist, with the traits he has or should have, charisma, authority (see p. 68), casts the healer as more authoritarian than many psychotherapists would deem fit and proper. He ties his ideas to the underlying premise that all healing comes from God. He quotes the French surgeon Ambrose Pare: "God heals the wound, I merely dress it" (p. 64). As noted above, his perception can lead to grave misunderstandings regarding the function of therapy and the role of the therapist.

Some theorists, expressing their views on the relation between Judaism and psychotherapy, have voiced opinions that, in certain aspects, are similar to Knight's position. Much has been written purporting to uncover the Jewish roots of psychotherapy. Some see a direct connection, whereas others dispute this. Such studies add an additional dimension to psychoanalytic and psychotherapeutic concepts and can illuminate rabbinical teachings. Others, however, present positions which, in effect, reduce religion to one primary aspect. Bakan,[7] for example, writes that psychoanalysis is a contemporary fulfillment of the style of religiosity that begins with Abraham. This statement, meant to be complimentary to Judaism, actually minimizes it by confining it to its humanistic feeling aspects. This trend of thought is similar to that of Erich Fromm[8] who proclaimed that only psychoanalysis is truly religious in the humanistic sense of the word religious. This thesis has been roundly criticized by the Harvard philosopher Bertocci[9] because it arbitrarily narrows the parameters of religion. Bakan's and Fromm's arguments are rooted in the liberal Protestant tradition which identifies religious life as moral life. Their position is not the Jewish perception which views religion as an all-encompassing way of life.

CONCEPTS COMMON TO BOTH JUDAISM AND PSYCHOTHERAPY: UNCONSCIOUS INNER FORCES

I wish to briefly present what seems to me basic and common to both Judaism and psychotherapy. This, of course, is my perception; there is no question but that others may differ. I've already noted in the opening pages of this book that the concept of the unconscious is not merely acceptable to the Judaic way of thought, but plays an integral part in understanding some aspects of Torah Judaism. In chapters 3 and 4 in my book (note no. 1), I discuss this concept at length. The differences between the Freudian model and that of Rabbi Israel Lipkins (Reb Yisroel Salanter) are pointed out and analyzed. Examples are presented showing how the concept can be utilized to explain the behavior of biblical personages as viewed by our sages and later rabbis, both Hasidic and non-Hasidic. Those chapters do not exhaust the examples which exemplify the workings of the unconscious. The dynamic concept of the unconscious has been criticized because it projects an image of man as an irrational being minimizing the intellect. It was shown there that this criticism is not justified and cannot be directed to the concepts promulgated by Rabbi Yisroel Salanter. In addition, the unconscious of Freudian theory, predicated on biology and drawing upon Darwinism, inevitably leads to its perception as a repository of hedonistic and aggressive instincts; this is not so for the "inner forces" of Rabbi Salanter, as discussed extensively in the two chapters.

Another aspect of the Salanterian concept is presented and discussed here. Dynamic psychology's explanation of the irrationality of the unconscious is that humans are inheritors of vestiges of primary process thinking. Primary process thinking is a Freudian concept; it is the mode of thought first used by humans. It does not follow the rules of logic and is rooted in the pleasure principle which dictates to the person that he/she follow only that which affords immediate pleasure. Rabbi Yisroel Salanter also postulated a relation between affect and reason. However, the link is not Freud's pleasure principle; it is the personality traits of the individual which influence the mode of thought. Different personality traits account for the diversity of cognitive perceptions and modes of thinking. The greatness of the revered Jewish sages lies in the fact that they were better able than others to nullify the traits exerted on their thinking process. The more uncompromised the intellect, the closer its reasoning approaches truth. He uses this principle to explain the controversy between the schools of the houses of Shamai and Hillel. The Talmuud relates that they argued for three years until a voice from heaven ("bas-kol") decreed that the decisions of the house of Hillel are to be followed and declared halachically correct. The "bas-kol" added that both opinions are considered the word of God. Rabbi Salanter explains this amazing statement by stating that obviously the opinions of the sages of both schools were arrived at by reasoning unsullied by their desires and purified of undesirable personality traits. This confers upon both opinions the status of the truth—Torah—despite the fact that they are contrary opinions. This apparent contradiction can be resolved by theological principles which, of course, is not the present intent of the author. What concerns us is the psychological philosophical principle that truth is arrived at by the uncompromised intellect. The question we must address is: How can it by that one group of sages held one opinion, while others equally eminent, held a conflicting opinion, despite the fact that both schools were not influenced by extraneous desires or wishes? Rabbi Salanter's explanation is that each group of scholars comprised people with similar personality traits which influence cognitive modes.[10]

This model suggests that differences of opinion between people are not necessarily the workings of irrationality. It can be understood as a result of different cognitive approaches whose roots stem from differing personality traits. It directs us to search for and examine personality traits as well as to delve into unconscious, in Salanterian terminology, "unclear" forces. The personality traits will help us understand the client's reasoning process, whereas analysis of the unconscious "unclear" forces and drives may uncover what is preventing the client from understanding himself, thereby distorting truth. This model has a close affinity to cognitive-based psychotherapy. It parts from the cognitive approach in that it includes the concept of the unconscious which alerts us to the possibility that the client may be unaware of his/her predispositions. Not being aware is what creates the power which influences the person to think and behave in certain ways.

SUBJECTIVITY-OBJECTIVITY

Judaism's emphasis on Halacha—Law—is well known and has been discussed by many thoughtful scholars. Of relevance to us is that its stress on norms, on clearly defined parameters of behavior, fosters a healthy esteem for objectivity. This does not permit the therapist to blindly follow the flights of his/her imagination-intuition which, at times, can be misleading. Intuition, the therapist's innermost feeling nurtured by years of experience, is an invaluable tool for the therapist, but can be misused to validate what is incorrect or untrue. Rampant subjectivity challenges the very idea of the existence of objective truth. Himmelfarb[11] writes, "The mainspring of post-modernism is a radical—and absolute, one might say—relativism, skepticism, and subjectivism that rejects not only the idea of the canon, and not only the idea of greatness, but the very idea of truth. For the postmodernist, there is no truth, no knowledge, no objectivity, no reason, and ultimately no reality." This harsh pronouncement is also correct for certain trends in psychotherapy which elevate subjectivity to be the prime factor in the therapeutic process. It is perhaps more than just a coincidence that the most central figure in the elevation of intuition in psychotherapy was Jung. He was reared in a religious environment which, unlike Judaism, does not have a detailed code of norms regulating everyday behavior. Consequently, the mystical intuitive aspects of religion formed his outlook which placed subjectivity and intuition on the highest plane. This fact may also explain his flirt with Nazi ideology, which it seems he later rejected. The romantic intuitive aspects of that ideology, which seemed to break out of the bounds of the mundane, old, and outworn schemas, may have appealed to his mode of thinking.

I often wonder as to whether Carl Rogers' basic premise of full nonjudgmental acceptance of the client is perhaps also a result of his subjective intuitive approach. He, too, was reared in a religious atmosphere which he abandoned. In his later years, he espoused certain psychotherapeutic practices, such as nude marathon psychotherapeutic sessions. The unconditional acceptance of the client which he espoused seems to mesh with his unconditional acceptance of any method which to him seemed to further honesty. This reflects an abandonment of all previously accepted norms, based solely on his subjective intuitive feelings. Perhaps his turning away from religion also led to his suspicion of other norms, as well. This extraordinary clinician blazed new trails, but in the process seems to have unnecessarily repudiated healthy psychological norms.

Rabbi Dr. Soloveitchik's critique of subjectivity was quoted in the first chapter. He discusses religion and philosophy, but his incisive comments and his reasoning justify transposing his comments to psychotherapy, as well. In one of his writings, he states that the schools of philosophy which venerate intuition and subjectivity "have brought complete chaos and human depravity to the world."[12]

An example of the detrimental effect of subjectivity on psychotherapy is discussed by Moustakas, a prominent psychologist.[13] He was a group leader in encounter groups. His style reflected his strong, but tender personality for which he was criticized. He, therefore, chose to adopt a more aggressive stance expressing anger quite frequently. He was successful, but began experiencing physical and emotional distress, leading him to revert to his previous mode of leadership. His analysis of what transpired distinguishes between honesty and truth. Honesty, in this context, meant giving vent to what is felt at a given moment, whereas truth represents a deeper, more permanent aspect of personality. Although Moustakas does not mention either objectivity or subjectivity, his understanding of honesty as expressing temporary feelings which are inconsistent with the "real" self of the person, in contrast to truth which is enduring and expresses one's most basic "self," can be viewed as subjectivity vs. objectivity. Subjectivity is fleeting and often governed by moods and irrelevant considerations, as opposed to objectivity which is bound to clear-cut criteria and not given to temporary aberrations. Judaism's commitment to Halacha is consonant with a frame of reference in psychotherapy which critically examines subjectivity, carefully balancing it with objectivity.

Extreme subjectivity in therapy is problematic from yet another angle. Subjectivity focuses one's thoughts and feelings on the self. The therapist who relies to an exaggerated extent on intuition overemphasizes the self to the exclusion of others. The message delivered by the therapist's behavior is that one's overriding concern should be the self. One's feelings should be the deciding factor guiding behavior. This is incompatible with Judaism which teachers that the other's well-being is as important as one's own: "Thou shalt love thy neighbor as thyself" (Leviticus, 9-18). Therapeutic methodology based on subjectivity bolsters the approach which views the self and its needs as supreme. Probing the client's feelings in a way that emphasizes their extreme importance, the constant reference by the therapist to his/her own feelings, delivers the message that the self and its needs are so paramount that it seems to be the only factor to be considered. This critique does not apply to the concept of the self as a construct, as a tool for understanding personality; the intent is to object to overemphasizing the self, viewing its welfare as the sole criterion on which to base one's behavior.[14]

SELF-KNOWLEDGE

Self-knowledge is a central component of both Judaism and psychotherapy. Singer[15] writes: "Psychotherapy is dedicated precisely to this aim, to make man comprehensible to himself, to help man fearlessly see himself, and to help him learn that this process of self-recognition, far from producing contempt, implies and brings about the achievement of dignity and self-fulfillment." Self-knowledge means recognizing one's motivations, desires, goals, and the subterfuges, the self-deceptions one practices to mask the truth from others and, more importantly, from oneself. This knowledge and the taking of steps to rectify the situation is, according to Singer, the essence of depth psychotherapy.

The importance of self-knowledge is recognized as well by academic social psychology which has researched the topics of self-understanding, self-awareness, and self-justification very extensively. Their studies have generated many theories; for example, self-evaluation maintenance theory, self-affirmation theory, self-verification theory, all explaining the complicated process we use to explain our actions to ourselves and to others. The research has spotlighted the pitfalls obstructing true self-perception. Aronson, Wilson, and Akert refer to the "illusion of freedom which characterizes so much of our decision-making process."[16]

This emphasis on self-knowledge is mirrored in the importance attached to it by Jewish thinkers. Bachya Ibn Pakudah, in his classic "Duties of the Heart" (Chovas Halevovot), writes that philosophy is man's knowledge of himself. The understanding of one's physical, emotional, and spiritual self will reveal Divine wisdom (Shaar Habechina, Gate 2, Chapter 5). He quotes Job (19:26): ". . . and from my flesh I'll perceive God" as proof of his thesis.[17]

Rabbi Avrohom Grodzinskii of Slobodka[18] who was killed in the Shoah (Holocaust) develops the thesis that without an understanding of the inner workings of personality, one cannot comprehend Torah teachings. The Torah prefaces many commandments—mitzvot—with the statement that fulfilling them will impress upon the doer the remembrance of epochal historical events, such as the redemption from Egypt and the miracles which took place during the forty years of wandering in the desert (Exodus, 12:14, 42; 13:9, 10; 23:14; Leviticus, 23: 43; Deuteronomy, 8:2). Notwithstanding the many reminders, we are cautioned not to be haughty (Deuteronomy, 8:14) because haughtiness causes forgetfulness. The Torah presents it as an axiom; it does not differentiate between individuals blessed with an excellent memory and those who are not similarly fortunate. It is obvious, reasons Rabbi Grodzinski, that the issue is not memory per se; rather the workings of the mind are so constructed, so put together, that seemingly extraneous factors, such as one's haughtiness, can and do influence memory.[19]

COMPLEXITY IN JUDAISM AND PSYCHOTHERAPY

A major premise of depth psychology is that human behavior is complex and multi-layered. This is due to the diverse factors, conscious and unconscious, which exert their influence on the person, directing his/her actions. Judaism also views behavior as complex and intertwined, as pointed out above. Depth psychology sees psychology as akin to archeology, a layer is uncovered—a deeper level is exposed. The acronym "pardes" (p'shat, remez, drash, and sod) is a well-known description of the conceptualization of Torah into four methods of interpretation. Torah is also described as having 70 faces (Gra, Eliyhu, the Gaon of Vilna, in his commentary on King Solomon's Shir Hashirim, Song of Songs). The need for differing levels of interpretation and the purpose they serve indicate that human behavior is complex; therefore, the methodology of interpretation needs to be complex, as well, to be able to correctly assess the myriad nuances of personality.

Rashi's comments based upon the sages' teachings on the word "vayichad" (Exodus, 18:9) illustrate the above principle. "Vayichad" conveys Yithro's reaction to his son-in-law's (Moses) description of the punishment meted out to the Egyptians. Moses recounted the details of Israel's redemption from Egypt, including the parting of the Red Sea and the drowning of the pursuing Egyptian army. Rashi presents two meanings for "vayichad": one (p'shat) Yithro rejoiced; the other (drash), he was chagrined—literally, his flesh crept with horror. The Torah deliberately chose this word; the usual translation of joy is "yismach." "Vayichad" was used precisely because of its ambiguity, which is designed to convey Yithro's complex and ambivalent feelings. He was happy for Moses and Israel, but also felt, consciously or unconsciously, sorrow and hurt for the Egyptians, whose advisor, according to the sages, he had been for many years. This approach is similar to the reasoning employed by depth psychologists in therapy, for whom the concept of the unconscious is a major determinant of behavior.

The confluence of Judaism and depth psychology on this issue, the complexity of human behavior, and the mode of reasoning employed to unravel hidden meanings and nuances of behavior have led some to maintain that psychoanalysis owes a debt to Judaism. Jennings and Jennings feel that the Midrash, the non-Halachic writings of the Talmudic sages, displays the kind of reasoning employed by Freud: "Like psychoanalysis, Midrash is dedicated to explicating and clarifying origins."[20] They term the Midrash the unseen origins of psychoanalysis. This argument differs from that of Bakan's thesis that the content matter of psychoanalysis shows kabbalistic mystical roots.[21] Jennings and Jennings are referring to the reasoning process, not the content matter.

INNER CONFLICT

The phenomenon of inner conflict permeates every aspect of human nature and behavior. We are constantly and simultaneously drawn in diverse, often opposite directions. Consensus is lacking as to the nature of the conflict. Judaism (as do other religions) attaches major importance to the tension between the spiritual and corporeal; psychological theories and systems each have different conceptions of the nature of the conflict, but all seem to agree that conflict exists and is a constant and inherent part of human nature. This has important consequences for therapy. It is not sufficient to acquire intellectual knowledge of the complexity and intricacies of the workings of human nature. Emotional well-being calls for knowledge of one's feelings, sensations, and emotions; however, this knowledge extends beyond basic cognitive knowledge. It means an intimate acquaintance based on a balanced measure of both affect and cognition. Inner conflicts, which compel us to adopt a self-justification stance in order to maintain self-esteem, may lead us to suppression of our feelings and emotions. An individual must become proficient at recognizing his/her moods, reactions, and feelings.

Although Judaism's perception of the nature of inner conflicts differs from that of the various psychological theories, it attaches major significance to the role inner conflict plays. The Torah views people, including those who have reached high spiritual levels, as nevertheless bound to their material self and subject to constant tension between their spiritual and material selves.[22] This is why persuasive arguments intended to influence individuals to strengthen religious convictions or correct behavior need to be couched in language comprehensible and meaningful to the material self. The Passover seder exemplifies this principle. This most central of Jewish family rituals is grounded in mitzvot (commandments) and ceremonies that speak directly to the child in simple verbal language and richly symbolic rituals. Its important message is not articulated in language addressing the intellect.[23] The symbolism of the matzot—unleavened bread—and bitter herbs, the four cups of wine and other characteristics is easily comprehended by all.[24]

An additional example will further clarify this point. "And He afflicted thee, and suffered thee to hunger, and fed thee with Manna, which thou knewest not, neither did thy fathers know: that He might make thee know that man doth not live by bread only, but by everything that proceeds out of the mouth of the Lord doth man live" (Deuteronomy, 8:3). Rabbi Kotler[25] singles out the fact that God chose first to bring Israel to a state of hunger and only then did He provide Manna. Why was this procedure necessary? Would not the miracle of the daily-provided Manna be sufficient to impress upon Israel the message that He wished to impart? Rabbi Kotler, therefore, deduces that a message, a teaching message, is effective only when the receiver is keenly aware of his needs, whereupon the fulfillment of these needs can and will leave an indelible impression on the recipient. Merely witnessing a miracle, even one of such magnitude as providing sustenance for a period of 40 years for an entire nation numbering, according to Biblical sources, in the millions, is not capable of branding in consciousness the effect which God wished to attain. People are a blend of the spiritual and material; consequently, teaching has to address both components of the person.

OTHER ISSUES RELEVANT TO JUDAIC PSYCHOTHERAPY

It seems to me that a number of short discussions on issues which have riveted my attention for some time is a fitting conclusion to this chapter.

The first issue is that of the relation of those personality traits which historically have been associated with "good" character versus "poor" character. This is unchartered territory, insofar as it is related to psychotherapy. It seems more pressing now, since spiritual concerns are now considered legitimate to be inserted into the therapeutic process. Those personality traits to which I am referring (middot) traditionally were seen to have a very close association with spirituality. For example, becoming a kinder, gentler, less vindictive person is, at present, a process which is viewed as an integral part of religion and ethics, not so it would seem, of psychotherapy. Some psychotherapeutic schools claim that the therapy practiced by them causes people to become better and kinder. Notice should be made that, on the contrary, some argue that the therapy practiced by most schools of therapy tends to make people more selfish and self-centered.[26] The task of identifying psychological factors which mold personality, good character traits, and conversely poor character traits, and the subsequent task of creating a methodology for dealing with them is a task for the future. Firstly, it will have to be determined whether this is a psychological task employing classical psychological methods or whether it fits into the ethical-moral tradition. If, indeed, it will be found that this task can be handled under psychology's aegis, it seems reasonable that it will be part of spiritual psychotherapy. At present, the line separating emotional difficulties from undesirable character traits is fluid and unclear. This lack of clarity poses a problem having practical implications. When does a presenting case cease being an emotional problem and become a personality trait problem which may not be in the realm of psychotherapy? Stated differently, which factors ought to be present in order that the patient be accepted for psychotherapy and not be advised to turn to a clergyman or an expert in moral-ethical principles? I will address this issue in the following chapter.

At this point, I wish to return to the issue of subjectivity and, in a broader sense, to the importance of Halacha—clear objectively defined norms of behavior—as it is related to psychotherapy. So as not to be misunderstood or misinterpreted, this does not mean that an observant, Halachic psychotherapist is confined to treat only those whose norms conform to Halacha. It also does not imply that we, as observant Jews and psychotherapists, should have less empathy toward those who differ from us. On the contrary, our ideals should dictate to us, in no uncertain terms, that we regard all humans as God's creatures deserving of His love and concern, and most certainly of ours. The import of my message is that the psychotherapeutic process should not be infused and permeated with subjectivity and intuition to the extent that it overshadows rationality and clear thinking. Halacha and, indeed all law, foster a respect for norms, for behavior conforming to such norms. If an individual client does not conform to our norms, it is not in our domain to use our influence to mold him/her in our image. I have commented on this issue in the first chapter and am returning to it here in the context of my presentation of what is common to both Judaism and psychotherapy. Psychotherapy is not a vehicle to be used in an authoritative manner to unfairly influence the client-patient to conform to our values. The client is entitled to our empathy and respect, no matter what his/her ideals and his/her likes and dislikes are. Therapists must freely allow clients to choose their own values. As Richards and Bergin write (see chapter 1), therapists may, however, share with the patients the wisdom they have acquired about values when it is relevant to the patients' problems.

As noted, all laws function to instill proper norms, to educate. The rule of law is more than just a code which guides authorities as to which behavior is punishable. It forms our perception of right and wrong. An example of this is pointed out by Krauthammer.[27] He informs us that in the Netherlands, where voluntary suicide by patients suffering from an incurable disease is permitted, there are cases of physicians practicing involuntary euthanasia. He attributes this to the fact that doctors are not constrained by law. "The absolute ethical norm established since the time of Hippocrates—that doctors must not kill—was removed in the name of compassion, and the inevitable happened. Good, ordinary doctors, in their zeal to be ever more compassionate in terminating useless and suffering life, began killing people who did not even ask for it.

Once given power heretofore reserved to God, some exceeded their narrow mandate and acted like God." It seems axiomatic that psychotherapy is even more in need of clear guidelines than is medicine. The therapist is consulted in his/her role as an expert in mental health and is involved in issues which border on ethical concerns. The absence of a framework to guide the therapist is tantamount to saying that there aren't any barriers which should not be breached and that all inhibitions promote ill health. This can and does lead to flagrant violations of the basic ethical code, such as sexual exploitation by some therapists, ostensibly to help the patient overcome emotional difficulties.

NOTES

1. Psychotherapy: Its Relation to Biblical and Rabbinic Judaism (1997). Journal of Psychology and Judaism. Vol. 2, No. 3. Judaism and Psychology: Meeting Points (1999). Northvale, NJ/Jerusalem: Jason Aronson: Chapter 6. Halachic Judaism's Influence on the Practice of Psychotherapy (2000-2001). Journal of Psychology and Judaism. Vol. 24, No. 3.

2. I believe that this is how psychotherapy is viewed by the majority of therapists. Freud, for example, deemed it necessary to declare that a psychoanalyst need not necessarily be a physician. This implies that although it is a healing process, the nature of this healing does not require a physician's medical expertise.

3. Integrating Spirituality into Treatment. Miller, William R. Ed. (1999). Washington, DC: American Psychological Association. PP. 20-21.

4. Frank, Jerome D. (1974). Persuasion and Healing. New York: Schocken Books.

5. Maimonides (Rambam) refers to people who stray from Torah as sick people (Mishneh Torah, Laws of De'ot, Chapter 3 and in his introduction to Pirkai Avot—Sayings of the Fathers, Chapters 3 and 4). He directs them to wise men, scholars whom he calls "healers of the soul." He is not referring to those whom we now designate emotionally disturbed people. He it talking about people who are sick in the religious, spiritual, and moral sense of the term sick.

6. Knight, James A. (1986). In two chapters entitled: (a) "The Religio-Psychological Dimension of Wounded Healers," Chapter 3, and in Chapter 4, "Minister and Healer: Each as the Other," he probes the deeper spiritual meanings of both minister and physician. In, Psychiatry and Religion: Overlapping Concerns, Ed. Lillian H. Robinson, MD, Washington, DC: American Psychiatric Press, Inc. The quote in the text is on PP. 53 and 54. He quotes Christian Scripture (Mark 3:15) as the basis for this statement, "power to heal sickness and to cast out demons." This perception is in direct opposition to the Jewish perception of emotional illness and its alleviation. See Judaism and Psychology (note 1), P. 131, for a fuller discussion of this point.

7. David Bakan is quoted as saying this in a forum in which he participated. Psychology and Religion: A Contemporary Dialogue (1968). Ed. J. Havens, P. 96. Princeton, NJ: Nostrand.

8. Fromm, Erich (1950). Psychoanalysis and Religion. New Haven: Yale University Press. See Chapters 3 and 5 and P. 74 in the Bantam Books ed.

9. Bertocci, Peter A. (1971). Psychological Interpretations of Religious Experience: Research on Religious Development. A Comprehensive Handbook. Ed. M. P. Strommen, PP. 5-41. New York: Hawthorn Books. Dr. Bertocci, who was a friend of the famous psychologist Gordon Allport, presents a thoughtful analysis of a number of psychological interpretations of the religious experience.

10. See Goldberg, H. (1982). Israel Salanter: Text Structure, Idea. New York: Ktav Publishing House. See also my article of 2000-2001, Note 1.

11. Himmelfarb, G. (1997). Revolution in the Library. The Key Reporter 62(3), 2-5. This small scholarly journal is published by the Phi Beta Kappa Society. It publishes articles by prominent scholars.

12. Rabbi Soloveitchik (1983). Halakhic Man. Philadelphia. Jewish Publication Society, P. 141.

13. Moustakas, C. E. (1972). Loneliness and Love. Englewood Cliffs, NJ: Prentice-Hall. Chpater 7.

14. See Wallach, M., and Wallach, L. (1983). Psychology's Sanction for Selfishness. San Francisco. See also Freeman, W. H., Wicklund, R. A., & Eckert, M. (1992). The Self-Knower: A Hero under Control. New York/London: Plenum Press. These books, especially the first, criticize the premise which places the self as the apex, the supreme goal on which to base the direction of therapeutic intervention. I often wonder why the Wallach book, authored by prominent psychologists, has not attracted greater attention and discussion.

15. Singer, Erwin (1965). Key Concepts in Psychotherapy. New York: Random House. P. 65.

16. Aronson, E., Wilson, T. D., Timothy, D., and Akert, R. M. (1997). Social Psychology, 2nd ed. New York: Longman. P. 204.

17. See also Rabbi Avrohom's Ibn Ezra's commentary on Exodus, 31:18. Maharal of Prague's introduction to "Beer Hagolah." Rabbi Yeruchem Levovitz, "Daas Torah," Bamidbar PP. 72-74.

18. Rabbi A. Grodzinski (1978). Torat Avrohom. Bnai Brak. PP. 182-214.

19. The example presented herewith illustrates the Torah's insistence on complete honesty in examining one's motivation. It also exemplifies the role of the unconscious. Sarah overheard the angel's prediction that she would give birth. She laughed in apparent disbelief, for which she was reprimanded. When she denied that she had laughed, the Torah states starkly and simply: "Nay, but didst laugh" (Genesis, 18:15). The Hasidic master Rabbi L. Eiger explains that she was not aware that she had acted disrespectfully [Rabbi L. Eiger (1889/1970) Torat Emet, Vol. 1l. P. 11. Bnai Brak: Yahadut]. Sarah felt that the angel's prediction could not materialize because she felt unworthy. It should be remembered that the angel appeared as a human. The Torah, however, establishes that although on a conscious level her modesty dictated her actions, on a deeper level a measure of disbelief had caused her to laugh. Self-knowledge and self-awareness are not to be compromised.

20. Jennings, Jerry, and Jennings, Jane P. (1993). I Knew the Method: The Unseen Midrashic Origins of Freud's Psychoanalysis. Journal of Psychology and Judaism,

17:1, 51-75. See also Handelman, Susan (1981). Interpretation as Devotion: Freud's Relation to Rabbinic Hermeneutics. Psychoanalytic Review, 68:2, 201-218. Another researcher was also impressed by the similarity of Talmudic and psychoanalytic reasoning. See my discussion of Marlene Paley's article in my book (note 1, P. 128).

21. Bakan, David (1958). Sigmund Freud and the Jewish Mystical Tradition. Princeton, NJ: Van Nostrand.

22. See, for example, Bachyah Ibn Pakudas, Duties of the Heart, third gate, and the Hasidic classic Tanya, Chapters 9 and 10.

23. This sentence bears further explanation. The language of the Haggadah, the book from which the participants read during the seder, is simple and straightforward; nevertheless, it is Torah, the teachings of the sages. It, therefore, has many and varied interpretations.

24. Levovitz, Rabbi Yeruchem (1966). Daas Chochma Umussar, Vol. 1, PP. 112-116. New York: Daas Chochma Umussar Publications.

25. Kotler, Rabbi Aaron (1982). Mishnat Rebbi Aharon, Vol. 1, PP. 8-15. Jerusalem: Mochon Yerushalayim.

26. See Wallach and Wallach, note no. 14.

27. Krauthammer, C. (1996). First and Last. Do No Harm. Time Magazine, April 15, 1996, P. 47.

Chapter Three

Principles of Judaic Spiritual Psychotherapy

The preceding chapter described in broad strokes a psychotherapeutic approach based on uniquely Judaic philosophy and values, coupled with the methods of psychotherapy used by contemporary therapists. The very nature of Jewish concepts and values serves as an apt introduction and foundation of Jewish spiritual psychotherapy. In this chapter are detailed some of the methods which fit into the category of spiritual tools used by the author. Richards and Bergin[1] write that perusal of Scriptures is one of the basic tools used in theistic spiritual psychotherapy. I refer to the Bible and Talmudic literature, as well as to sayings and behavior of recognized sages throughout the centuries. The wisdom contained in the selections and sayings seems appropriate for use with non-Jewish and secular clients as well.

Every therapist has encountered people who, although not clinically depressed, are unhappy and consistently pessimistic. They always seem to see the black cloud in every lining and are difficult to live with. This is true even for some who are successful in their chosen professions. However, their expectations are such that they never feel that they are fulfilled, which causes them to regard themselves as below par and wanting. Psychotherapists have their methods which they follow: dynamic, behavioral, cognitive, Rogerian, etc. I prefer the dynamic coupled with cognitive methods meant to elucidate the meanings attached to the clients' use of words and interpretations of others' speech and behavior. I also attach great significance to the concept of self-image.

Rabbi Ahron of Karlin, one of the early Hasidic masters and the founder of the Hasidic sect known as Karlin-Stolin, taught his followers how to differentiate between atzvut—sadness, which is anathema to Hasidim, and merrirut—bittersweet feeling, which is praiseworthy. His denigration of sadness is shared by all Hasidim and, although not considered a sin—a transgression, is viewed as a state of mind, a personality trait, which can and does lead to grave breaches of Torah endangering and greatly undermining spirituality. The danger inherent in a situation where a person finds himself beset by such feelings is that he/she may be unaware of the true nature of the feelings. Rabbi Ahron (the great) proposed a simple test capable of determining the nature of the feelings. The person monitors his/her behavior; if these feelings cause the person to go to bed, to lie on his/her back and while away the time bemoaning the situation, then sadness—atzvut—is the culprit. If, however, the feelings engender a sense of purpose, a willingness to act constructively in a spiritual sense, then he/she is dealing with merrirut—bittersweet feelings, not a malignant despondency. Sharing this insight with the client and engaging him/her in a discussion of the premise and relating it to his/her experiences have proved to be a powerful tool in helping the client reframe his/her perceptions of what is transpiring and, perhaps even more importantly, is a first step in a change of self-image.

Often the despondency, the sadness, is accompanied by a feeling of worthlessness. The client feels that he or she is not a person deserving of God's beneficence. This is assumed by the client because of his/her self-perception as a sinner. This can be the case whether transgressions are real or imagined. In such instances, I often engage them in a conversation revolving around one of the Chofetz Chayim's teachings. Rabbi Israel Meir of Radin—the Chofetz Chayim, the acknowledged world leader of Judaism during the period after World War I. He lived a long and extraordinary life authoring many books which have guided and still guide Orthodox Jews, both in Halachic decisions and "Hashkofa"—how to perceive one's life and one's surroundings. He is called the "Chofetz Chayim" which is the title of the first book he published in the latter part of the 19th century. This consists of two parts, the first being an authoritative codex of the laws of slander; the second part consists of his elucidation of the teachings of the sages concerning the evil of slanderous speech. In the latter part, he explains at length what is recorded in the Bible (Numbers, 13 and 14). Moses sent 12 distinguished persons to reconnoiter the Promised Land. He asked them to investigate specific issues and return with answers and recommendations. Upon returning, they reported that it was indeed a bountiful land. However, they added that it would prove impossible to conquer, thereby denying that the Almighty is capable of dislodging the nations occupying the land. Their negative report sparked widespread unrest in the Israelites culminating in God's decision to have the nation, all males above 20 years of age, wander in the desert for 40 years. This, of course, meant that they would not enter the Promised Land. The exceptions among the 12 were Joshua and Caleb who had argued passionately that God's promise will be fulfilled and that there is no cause to worry and doubt its fulfillment. In the course of the arguments, the two implored "do not rebel against Him" (Numbers, 14:9). The Chofetz Chayim interprets this to mean that a person need not be an extraordinary righteous person to deserve God's favors. It is sufficient to be one who does not rebel.[2] The Chofetz Chayim reads the dialog between Joshua and Caleb and the other spies (and the Israelites who tended to side with the gloomy forecast) as follows: The others, who were distinguished leaders, claimed that the Israelites were unworthy and should therefore not expect God to render miracles to expel and conquer the seven nations inhabiting Canaan. To this came the retort that one need not be outstanding in righteousness to be the recipient of God's succor, merely not to rebel.

A Midrashic homily (Midrash Tanchuma, Deuteronomy, Aikev) can be cited to ease the burden of sinfulness and unworthiness. The Midrash analyzes the reason for God's love for Israel. The verses in the Bible (Deuteronomy, 7:7.8) tell us that the Almighty's love for Israel is not because they are numerous; on the contrary, Israel is the smallest of nations. His love is intrinsic and based upon His obligation by oath to the patriarchs. The Midrash interprets the phrase: "the smallest of nations" to mean their modesty and humility. The gentile world performs, so says the Midrash, more mitzvot—good deeds—than Israel, mitzvot which they are not obligated to keep (Gentiles are required to keep only seven commandments); the gentiles also spread God's word to the far corners of the earth. What, then, is that which binds the Almighty to Israel?—their modesty, the fact that Israel minimizes itself and its accomplishments. This homily instructs and teaches the person that even if he/she is wanting in fulfilling obligations (the Midrash uses the word "hagunim"—i.e., not as one should be), the humble modest person is beloved by the Almighty. This is conditional on the person's acceptance of God and His Torah.

The lesson learned from this remarkable dialog is that, although we should aspire to lofty spiritual heights, this is not to be understood as meaning that only attainment of such heights guarantees us God's love and help. Every person who basically accepts God and does not rebel is assured of Divine grace and succor. This lesson, it seems to me, affects clients in two ways. It teaches us that (1) we are not as unworthy as we at times see ourselves, in spite of our failures and transgressions; and (2) our feelings are shared by others, our self-doubts are not unique to us, and we can and should gauge ourselves as worthy of His love and care.

The therapeutic interchange described above can be followed with a citation of the Gra, Rabbi Eliyhu (Elijah) of Vilna.[3] He interprets the sages' teaching which is based upon the verses in Job 33:23,24. The verses inform us that even if only one angel speaks well of an individual, his opinion is accepted in spite of the fact that 999 other angels speak ill of him. The Talmud

(Tractate Shabas 33:A) understands this to refer also to an instance where 999 "parts" of the single angel speak ill and the one remaining part speaks well. The Gra interprets this as meaning the following. Each good deed that a person performs gives birth to an angel. Not all good deeds can be classified as exceedingly pure, as having been motivated solely by the desire to please the Almighty. A person's actions can and are often motivated by ulterior reasons; for example, by seeking respect from his fellow humans. According to the Gra, the sages, therefore, tell us that even in instances where the motivating force for performing the mitzvah was 999 part impure, the remaining one part suffices to consider the person as being righteous and deserving of God's mercy.

The potency of the Chofetz Chayim's and the Gra's teachings cannot be overestimated. It brings to mind the sages noting that God's goodness is 500 times greater than His displeasure.

An additional insight to be learned from the above is that, in spite of our transgressions, we are worthy of God's mercy and love and that it can mitigate the feeling of inadequacy we may experience as to our meager spiritual accomplishments. This feeling can haunt us and nullify our wish to be close to Him. We take stock of ourselves, review our knowledge of Torah, our devotion to walking in His ways, our joy in performing His mitzvot. This process leaves us frustrated, consequently lowering our motivation to improve. We see our attainments as miniscule and deficient. There is no question but that the essence of spiritual growth is a constant desire to grow, to expand one's knowledge and commitment. However, we are taught that at the same time our meager accomplishments need not and should not dampen our spirits to the extent that it causes additional descent into worldliness, farther away from spirituality. This idea is developed by proponents of the Mussar school founded by Reb Yisroel Salanter (Rabbi Israel Lipkin), as explained in the following paragraph.

One of the leading Talmudists of the Middle Ages, Rabbi Asher, whose Talmudic commentaries and Halachic decisions are a prime component of the "Shulchan Oruch," the code of Jewish law, also wrote Urchos Chayim. These are short, concise teachings meant to guide himself and others in day-to-day behavior. This small volume was divided by Rabbi Heller, the author of "Tosfot Yom Tov" on the Mishnayot into seven parts, each part to be recited on a day of the week. In the sayings of Wednesday (No. 69), loosely translated: "Wish or yearn for what your Creator wishes, be satisfied with your position whether small or large." The Mussar masters[4] write, that as is commonly accepted, each person has a specific purpose for which he or she is created. This has to be accomplished during the person's lifetime. The "yetzer," the evil in the world, attempts to hinder, to block this accomplishment. The person is, of course, instructed to do all in his/her power to attain the goal cut out for him/her. One cannot ask why Mr. or Mrs. X is expected to expend energy on a certain task, whereas his/her friend has a different task, perhaps more difficult, or, on the contrary, easier. These speculations cannot be answered by mortal humans. The person's task is to accomplish his/her purpose, to overcome the difficulties, not to bemoan either his/her fate or the dearth of his/her spiritual accomplishments which may be diminished due to the nature of the task. They add that understanding this premise leads the person toward serenity.

This sage piece of advice from the masters of the Mussar school is most useful when the client feels that had he been granted more congenial circumstances to facilitate his spiritual growth, he would have attained greater knowledge and a deeper, more profound sense of closeness to Torah and God. The wisdom and empathy expressed in the Rabbi's interpretation turn the issue around. Our sole concern is no longer to constantly review our attainments and thereby measure our level of spirituality. We are also enjoined to eradicate the evil in us and in our surroundings so that we can accomplish the task our Creator mapped out for us. Let us, for example, imagine a situation where a promising young scholar is forced by unusually difficult circumstances to consider terminating his studies. This, of course, is not a simple decision and his teachers and other Halachic authorities must be consulted. However, since such situations do occur, the individual must know that what is expected of him/her, from a spiritual point of view, is that which the Almighty now wishes him/her to do.

We are taught that people are expected and required to utilize their abilities as best and as fruitfully as possible. This applies to the circumstances, the situation they find themselves in, as well as to their natural abilities. Rabbi Yisroel Salanter who, as noted above, was the founder of the Mussar Movement and arguably, perhaps, the greatest Talmudic giant and saintly person of his generation, is quoted as saying the following to his student, the noted Rabbi Naftali Amsterdam. Rabbi Naftali is reported (it seems on the Purim festival) to have said to his teacher: "If only I had your intellectual prowess and sterling character traits" (and then went on to mention particular attributes of other Talmudic giants) . . . "I would have advanced much further in my spiritual attainments." Rabbi Yisroel then gently chided him: "Naftali, you with your abilities are required to attain great heights commensurate with those abilities and that is what is expected of you by the Almighty."

The issues raised and the subsequent discussions revolve around the concepts of guilt and self-image. They are either affected by the person's actions or are the cause of his/her behavior. Guilt and a negative self-image may stem from many factors; their roots may lie in the early history of the individual and must be explored. Spiritual psychotherapy's contribution is that it broadens the parameters of the inquiry and adds depth to our understanding of the emotions engendered. Usually the therapist deals with the effects of a transgression reported by the client which shatters his self-image and lowers his self-esteem.

An interesting variation is when a client seems to misread the severity of his/her actions, his/her reported transgressions, insofar as they reveal his/her personality. This occurs when the client's level of self-understanding is deficient.

A young scholar, a God-fearing individual, was subjected to an extended traumatic emotional upheaval caused by marital familial difficulties. In the course of therapy, he reported with sorrow two religious transgressions: one of a sexual nature, the other a willful desecration of the Sabbath. He regarded the former as the greater sin. He was so utterly imbued with the idea of sexual purity that desecrating the Sabbath seemed relatively minor. To the therapist, it seemed quite clear that the sexual sin was an outgrowth of a long repressed natural instinct. The therapist did not minimize the severity of that behavior, but felt that in spite of its gravity, it can be understood as exhibiting a natural physiological trait and, although it certainly should have been repressed and not done, nevertheless was within the bounds of normal behavior. This was evaluated so in contrast to the Sabbath desecration which was knowingly and willfully done, and exhibited a deep sense of anger at the Almighty, manifested in a rebellious act of defiance. It proved exceedingly difficult for the client to grasp this. This was important because, although he was an intelligent person, it revealed his weakness regarding emotional intelligence, specifically, how his sense of values colored and influenced his perception of his actions. The therapy included a thorough discussion of the issue of the relative severity of sin, stressing the importance attached to actions dictated by rebellious acts of defiance.

The clients whose cases were alluded to suffer from a sense of unworthiness. This state of affairs is not the only kind therapists practicing spiritual psychotherapy have to deal with. We may be faced with a client who exudes smugness, a sense of self-satisfaction. Indeed, if this feeling does not impinge on other areas of his/her emotional stability, we question whether this should concern us. However, it would seem that in most situations this sense of smugness evolves into, or perhaps is, a result of a basic self-centeredness which is not a healthy situation from either a psychological or Judaic point of view.

To avoid misunderstanding, it cannot be emphasized too strongly that we are expected, instructed, to channel all our abilities and energies, every fiber of our physical, mental and emotional being, to the primary reason for our existence, which is to serve the Almighty, to hearken unto His Torah. The lesson gleaned from the foregoing sages' comments is that we humans can find ourselves bound to certain situations and circumstances which are not conducive to spiritual growth. These kinds of situations are not be bemoaned; they are to be perceived as clearly showing what the Almighty expects of us in the particular situation. This is His will, His way of testing us, His way of declaring that these situations are to be viewed as instruments with which to serve Him.

Rabbi Kanivesky's[5] interpretation of a "posuk"—a verse, can serve to clarify what may for some be difficult to comprehend. The Stipler—that is how Rabbi Kanivesky is commonly known—comments on a verse in Proverbs, 24:16. Loosely translated: "A righteous person will trip and fall seven times and rise up." This verse is understood by all to refer to a spiritual situation. A Torah life is not static; it has its high points and low points. This is what Proverbs teaches. The Stipler poses the question: Why is this so? Why does a God-fearing person have moments when he/she is connected to the Almighty and Torah and at other times seems to descend to a more materialistic existence. The Stipler's explanation is a novel psychological analysis. Humans are dissatisfied with their material acquisitions; they always want more. The Talmud says that he who has a hundred desires two hundred. However, the craving for spirituality is not that intense; with time we can be satisfied with just a bit, a smattering of spirituality. This leads to a lackadaisical performance of mitzvot—the Almighty's commandments. This realization can prod the person to awaken as if from a stupor and cause him/her to redouble his/her efforts in the spiritual realm. This, the Stipler maintains, is the benefit gained from the ascents and descents of the righteous person. A person who internalizes this concept finds renewed energy enabling him/her with increased vigor to pursue his/her spiritual goals. The insight which is imbibed is: Face the difficulties, see in them the potential for growth, and follow that path.

The psychotherapeutic benefits of these lessons are an invigorated sense of purpose and a healthier, more balanced positive self-image. These can be further fostered by a discussion of an extraordinary saying of Rabbi Zadok[6] of Lublin, a highly respected Talmudic giant and Hasidic master. He writes: "Just as one has to believe in the Almighty—he, the person, has to believe in himself, i.e., that the Almighty loves him and sees him as a worthy being." The phrase, to believe in oneself, placing it after belief in God, is indeed a powerful expression of a person's intrinsic worth.

The following concept can perhaps serve as a summary encapsulating the lessons expounded upon above. The basic thought is that banality and moral failures found in people are not to be viewed as reflecting the reality of the individual, the authentic person. The "evil inclination" is not the totality of the person. Judaism teaches that humans have two souls: the earthy and the spiritual (Tanya, Chapter 9, Rabbi Shneur Zalman, the founder of Lubavitch, Chabad). They are inimical to one another and are in constant conflict. The earthy soul and the evil inclination are not the entire, I. Rabbi Elijah of Vilna (Gra) teaches that the "person," the "I" is the "ruach" (spirit). This is a segment of the soul (neshama) that is entrusted with the power of choice and is prone to be influenced by one of the two inclinations. This approach facilitates the client seeing himself or herself as a basically worthy person. See my chapter in *Casebook for a Spiritual Strategy in Counseling and Psychotherapy*, Eds. Richards and Bergin, APA, 2004), in which I describe a case where the client was helped when this concept was discussed with him (p. 139).

Rabbi Yeruchem Levovitz's[7] analysis of the tests which the patriarch Abraham was subjected to teaches us an extraordinary fact about the complexity of human personality. Abraham was tested 10 times, the last time being asked to sacrifice his beloved son, Isaac. This request is considered the most difficult task of the 10 tests. Rabbi Yeruchem poses the question, accepting this fact: Why, then, was Abraham tested 10 times? Would not passing the last, most difficult task have been sufficient to show his devotion to the Almighty? His explanation probes the recesses of human personality. Often we are acquainted with a person who eminently qualifies to be considered highly spiritual, so much so that he towers above others. The onlookers attempt to evaluate him and learn from his fine traits. However, it sometimes happens that close scrutiny of the individual may reveal a major flaw in the person's character. There is a natural tendency to attempt to reconcile what is a fissure between various aspects of the person's character. It is difficult to accept that the person is not an integrated, well-balanced individual. Rabbi Levovitz informs us that we are mistaken. This is human. One can be admirable in many traits and, simultaneously in another aspect, be unworthy of our admiration, exhibiting a negative trait. This exemplifies the complexity of human character and behavior, as discussed in the previous chapter.

Rabbi Yeruchem's grasp of the intricate workings of personality is demonstrated in another of his discourses. He refers to a Midrashic teaching which says that Dina, the patriarch Jacob's daughter, at first refused to be liberated from the house of Shechem who had abducted her. Rabbi Yeruchem attributes this to the power of persuasion. True, she was taken by force from Jacob's house, from the highest level of spirituality, to that of Shechem, certainly not a home which radiated goodness and a spiritual mode of life. Nevertheless, such is the power of persuasion, of sweet talk, that Dina was for a short time bewitched and led astray. A person's steadfastness, of holding on to principles though thick and thin, can be fragile at times. To illustrate this point, Rabbi Levovitz asks us to imagine ourselves entering a store to buy cloth. The salesman shows us material, but the buyers (we) are not pleased. The salesman does not let up; he removes other cloths from the shelves, all the time extolling the virtues of each cloth, its reasonable price, etc. The buyer is well aware that the salesman is not telling the truth. Nevertheless, the constant flow of words, the assurances of the salesman have an effect, leaving a favorable impression. Slowly, but surely, the buyer is convinced and leaves with the merchandise. We may know that we have been misled; nevertheless, such is the power of speech.

Rabbi Yeruchem buttresses his argument by citing what is related in Genesis, 14:22. After Abraham rescued the King of Sodom, he was requested by the king, who wished to express his gratitude, to keep for himself the monies, etc. which Abraham was able to retrieve from the enemies of Sodom. Abraham refused and swore that he would not accept any recompense. Why, asks Rabbi Yeruchem, did Abraham have to swear? He had already emphatically declared that he would not consider a financial reward. The explanation that Rabbi Yeruchem proposes is that Abraham was fully aware of the power, the potency of persuasion. His method of coping with this was by swearing. The sages taught that the righteous are accustomed to swearing to rein in their desires.

The emotional impact of these stories lies in its making the client aware of his/her humanity, to view him/herself as part of the vast majority of people who are subjected to all kinds of influences and persuasions. He learns to see him/herself as behaving as most people do. This bolsters his/her sense of belonging and his/her self-image. Even the patriarch Abraham has to undergo ten tests, each task focusing on a different aspect of Abraham's character. Judging from an isolated incident, notwithstanding the enormity of the incident, we cannot assume that we know everything about the person. We humans are complicated creatures; therefore, we have to continually work to understand and improve ourselves while at the same time being aware of our complexity and imperfections. This is the essence of being human.

Nachaminides (Ramban) teaches us a basic psychological principle illuminating the workings of the human mind and psyche. He interprets the verse (Deuteronomy, 29-19) as stating that if an individual overindulges in following his natural instincts as, for example, sexual promiscuity, he will then wish to fulfill his desires in other ways, such as homosexuality and relations with animals. This is an extraordinary powerful teaching and further research is called for to ascertain its usefulness in psychotherapy. He postulates this principle for all manners of desire.

A major component of psychological disintegration is the feeling of the client whose presenting symptom is a pervading sense of unworthiness that all is lost, that what transpired cannot be repaired; hope has vanished. The Judaic response centers on the concept of teshuva—literally returning (to God)—repentance. An entire month-and-a-half of the Jewish calendar, including two major holidays, is devoted to this concept: the last month of the year, "Elul," and half of the first month "Tishrei"—Rosh Hashanah commencing the new year and Yom Kippur, the Day of Atonement. It is significant that the new year is celebrated and observed as a day of judgment. The holiday aspect is a result of the fact that standing in judgment, praying to Him, is a measure of closeness to the Almighty. Both Rosh Hashanah and Yom Kippur revolve around teshuva on a communal and personal level. The sages teach that teshuva—repentance—was created prior to the creation of the world. Repentance permeates every fiber of a person. A prayer beseeching God to accept our repentance is a permanent part of each of the three main prayers recited each day. Its importance, its centrality rings forth from the Bible. It is part and parcel and a major component of the prophecies.

Rabbi Aharon Kotler[8] presents us with an interesting and unique understanding of Rosh Hashanah, the holiday at the start of the new year. As noted above, the holiday is the time when the Almight judges all humankind. It also is the beginning of the ten days of repentance which culminate on the fast day of Yom Kippur—the Day of Atonement. In a well-detailed lecture, Rabbi Kotler writes that on the holiday of Rosh Hashanah, a person should not concern himself with his past, with the transgressions committed—this in spite of the fact that the holiday is one of the ten days of repentance. The day of judgment should be focused on reviewing one's pledge of accepting God's sovereignty. On this awesome day, the person should view himself as born anew; it is a new beginning unburdened by misdeeds of the past. The process of examining one's actions and cleansing oneself of the blemishes is commenced only after one's subservience to God is renewed and strengthened. Repentance means experiencing a deep feeling of regret, taking upon oneself a firm commitment to better one's actions and thoughts. This refers primarily to transgressions against the Almighty's precepts. If a person sinned against his fellow man, then in addition to the above, the wrongdoer has to set things right with the wronged party. The therapeutic benefit is that, aside from repenting, a fresh start is within reach of every person.

The following is an additional example of the efficacy of spiritual counseling. A person who is engrossed in a spiritual endeavor, for example, prayer, may paradoxically after reciting the prayer, experience a descent into negative behavior, instead of a spiritual uplifting. This seemingly strange situation has been foreseen by some Hasidic masters.[9] They describe the following scenario. A person's prayers are imbued with deep love for the Almighty. This love may subsequently be transformed into mundane profane love. In the event that the prayers are recited with awe, with a fear of the Lord, the feeling can sometimes undergo metamorphosis and emerge as short-temperedness or anger. This situation can be rectified by engaging in Torah study or some sort of constructive physical engagement. Acquainting the client with this homily puts him at ease with his predicament and with himself.

In the second chapter, I have discussed very briefly the relation of character traits to psychotherapy. It was noted that spiritual psychotherapy seems fitted to deal with failing character traits (middot). I am now returning to this issue. The dilemma we are faced with is that, in clinical practice, it is not an easy task to determine the line dividing psychotherapy and moral ethical guidance. For example, when is a presenting problem considered psychological and a candidate for psychotherapy, as opposed to viewing it as a moral ethical issue to be addressed by other means and other individuals? Furthermore, even when the basic difficulty is clearly psychological, there often are intertwining issues which belong to the category of "middot"—personality character traits.[10]

This dilemma is due partly to the lack of clarity as to the criteria defining emotional pathology. What exactly differentiates between flawed character traits (middot raot) and pathology? When, for example, should narcissistic behavior be viewed as reflecting emotional pathology rather than exemplifying egotism and selfishness? A logical starting point for such an analysis would seem to be an examination of the conditions which have to be present so as to exempt the perpetrator from his/her responsibility. When is he or she held culpable and deserving of punishment? The Judaic position that only a "shoteh"—a demented person—whose actions are patently illogical and irrational is not considered responsible for his/her behavior, would seem to exclude non-psychotic behavior.[11] It, therefore, follows that negative behavior rooted in faulty character traits are punishable. This established, it leads us to declare that the traits which spawned this behavior are not emotional problems, but are an ethical moral issue. However, an additional relevant Judaic principle has to be considered.

The sages teach that the verse in Psalms (Tehillim) that the Almighty tests a righteous person means that God tests only if it is certain that the person tested is capable of resisting the temptation, of emerging victorious from the encounter.[12] This threshold is not uniform; it differs from person to person. It, therefore, follows that evaluation and judgment of behavior are relative, not absolute. True, there is no distinction between people as to their obligation to heed the Torah's commandments; however, there is no universal scale of rewards and punishments equally applicable to all.[13] The Talmud states that God judges the actions, the behavior of the righteous more stringently than the behavior of others.[14] Another teaching of the sages is that Divine reward is meted out commensurate with the difficulties faced in the performance of the mitzvah—commandment (Lepum Tzaara Igra). This refers principally to external obstacles. However, it is applicable as well to the internal obstacles which are a result of emotional disturbance.[15]

Having established that, God expects a higher level of conduct from the righteous and that the measure of responsibility is dependent upon the person's spiritual level, we can now postulate that emotional difficulties, which naturally affect one's spiritual level, are important factors influencing Divine reward and retribution. Personality theorists should seek to establish criteria which can differentiate between behavior caused by emotional difficulties from that stemming from flawed character traits which traditionally have been associated with morality and ethical values. The crux of the argument presented here is that the development of therapeutic spiritual psychotherapy, or as Richards and Bergin term it—theistic therapy—paves the way toward a resolution of the dilemma. Injecting spiritual values into the psychotherapeutic process blurs the traditional distinction between psychotherapy and moral ethical guidance. Great care and caution, however, must be exercised so as not to confuse the two. Notwithstanding the merging to a certain extent of the two, they are nevertheless distinct and autonomous disciplines.

Psychological pain may be rooted in (a) either the client's dissatisfaction with his/her fulfillment of religious obligations or (b) situations where the presenting problem does not have discernible religious characteristics, but nevertheless hints at spiritual aspects that bear examining. Spiritual psychotherapy utilizes spiritual and theistic material and insights culled from religious sources which can be used in the therapeutic encounter. It is self-evident that this therapy is not intended to bolster religious beliefs; its purpose is to alleviate emotional pain using spiritual content material.

A word or two of caution is in order. Therapists should not expect spiritual therapeutic counseling to be a panacea. I concur with Blazer's critique of popular books on Christian counseling.[16] Blazer is a fundamentalist Christian psychiatrist. He feels that the books propose facile formulas to deal with psychopathology, particularly depression. He writes, "The ancient writers (Scripture) expressed and empathized with persons suffering emotional pain. Biblical writings are filled with wisdom relevant to the depressed in the modern era, however, no formulas were provided to guarantee freedom from depression." He also criticizes our society which demands instant gratification, including the right to emotional well-being. This has been discussed and analyzed by Rabbi Dr. Soloveitchik.[17] "The popular ideology contends that the religious experience is tranquil and neatly ordered, tender and delicate . . . if you wish to acquire tranquility without paying the price of spiritual agonies, turn unto religion . . . this ideology is intrinsically false and deceptive. That religious consciousness in man's experience which is most profound and most elevated . . . is not simple and comfortable. On the contrary, it is exceptionally complex, rigorous, and tortuous. Where you find its complexity, there you find its greatness."

NOTES

1. Richards, P. Scott and Bergin, Allan E. (1997). A spiritual Strategy for Counseling and Psychotherapy. Washington, DC: American Psychological Association, PP. 207-211.
2. Chofetz Chayim. Shmirat Holoshen, second part. Comments on Parshat Shlach.
3. Gra. Commentary on Proverbs 16-1.
4. Urchos Chayim Larosh Hamevuar, Bnai Brak, 2000. Commentaries of Rabbis Levovitz and Levenstein.
5. Birchas Peretz, Bnai Brak, 1990. PP. 53-54.
6. Rabbi Zodok of Lublin, Zidkut Hatzadik. Reprinted many times. Saying no. 154.
7. Rabbi Yeruchem Levovitz. Daat Torah, Vol. 1. Bereshit (Genesis). Jerusalem, 1986. See PP. 136 and 211. Rabbi Levovitz's basic premise that a person of sterling quality character traits may nevertheless have a major negative trait brings to mind the famous Milgram experiments. Stanley Milgram demonstrated that normal decent college students can exhibit cruel traits under given circumstances. Students who acted as jailers in a psychological experiment began to show cruelty to other students who acted as prisoners.
8. Rabbi Aaron Kotler (1998). Mishnas Rebbi Ahron, Ethical discourses, Vol. 2, PP. 183-184. See also Rabbi Doniel Movshovitz (2002) in Kisvai Hasaba M'Kelm, Talmiduv, Vol. 2. Bnai Brak, P. 762 (Yiddish). Reb Doniel, who perished in the Holocaust, views Rosh Hashanah as the gate to Yom Kippur. Teshuva, repentance (Yom Kippur) can be realized only if the person is acquainted with and bound to the Almighty. Neglecting formation of this bond negates repentance. Rosh Hashanah creates and forms the bond.
9. See Degel Machne Ephraim by the Baal Shem Tov's grandson, Parshat Ki Tisa. He quotes the Baal Shem Tov's student, Rabbi Yaakov Yosef of Polonia.
10. See the "Cure of Souls, Science, Values and Psychotherapy" (1998), Robert L. Woolfolk, San Francisco: Jossey-Bass. Reviewed in *Contemporary Psychology*, June, 1999, Vol. 44, No. 3. On page 5, the author argues that therapy is "analogous to what in other times has been called the cultivation of character."
11. The sages taught that a person sins only if and when a disturbed muse—ruach shtus—prods him to do so. This, however, does not minimize the sinner's culpability.
12. Psalms 11:5. The sages' interpretation is in the Midrash, Berashit Rabba, 32.
13. Psalms 50:3. The sages' comments are in Tractates Baba Kama 50:A and Yevomot 121:B.

14. The renowned Rabbi Chayim of Volozhin ties this concept to the fact, proclaimed by the Kabbalists, that the souls (neshamot) of individuals differ. It seems that some are rooted in greater innate spirituality than others. See Baurai Rabbainu Chayim Mevelozhin, 1985. Jerusalem: P. 65.

15. The principles enunciated in the text lead to a profound interpretation of the mechanics of divine reward and punishment. Rabbi Chayim of Volozhin (see previous note) writes that actions of a particular individual may be, due to his/her more spiritual soul, more severely criticized than the behavior of a different individual, who was not granted a neshama (soul), as pure as the first person. This is so, explains Rabbi Chayim, because the first person's actions, his transgressions, create a greater spiritual blemish having repercussions in the entire universe than others not so blessed. It follows that similar conduct by two individuals may be judged differently. See also Torat Hamagid, Rabbi Ber M'Mezritch, Bnai Brak, P. 45, where the same principle is alluded to. See also Mishant Rebbi Aharon (1988), Vol. 2. Lakewood, NJ: PP. 27-30.

16. Blazer, Dan G. (1998). Freud vs. God. Illinois: Inter-Varsity Press.

17. Rabbi Dr. Soloveitchik, J. B. (1983). Halakhic Man. Philadelphia: Jewish Publication Society of America, P. 141.

Chapter Four

Methodology

REFINEMENT OF THE METHOD: CASE HISTORIES

Further clarification of the issue of character traits and psychotherapy is illustrated by the following case histories. The examples are similar in that their problems are closely related to the special niche their families occupied in the religious social hierarchy. One client was a descendent of a prominent Hasidic family, the second traced his lineage to highly respected scholars. One was in his thirties, the other in his twenties. Both were happily married and devoted fathers. They felt that their distress was related to the family's social position. One felt that his family was being harassed by former friends who believed that the client was disrespectful of his family's tradition. He can be perceived a victim of unfortunate circumstances. He did not know how to cope with the situation and became frustrated and slightly depressed. During the two sessions we met, he dwelled on his misfortune. My impression was that he expected me to comfort him. He did not return for further sessions. My assessment was that he divined my intention to discuss the religious implications of not accepting the situation, of not gracefully acknowledging God's intent and will. His frustration is not difficult to understand and empathize with; he stood to lose a respected, powerful position and it was not an easy task to accept this. The problem that I, as the therapist faced, is whether his difficulties are rooted in his psychic makeup? Are we dealing with a weak ego which cannot cope with misfortune? Or is it a matter of pride or perhaps even avarice? In psychological terms, his situation can be perceived as a blow to his narcissism—or pride. My understanding of his terminating the therapy is that the intended therapeutic approach stressing spiritual-religious aspects may have unnerved and intimidated him. Facing defects in the religious sphere, not accepting that his predicament is the Almighty's doing, may have been more traumatic for him than facing psychological blemishes.

The second client, Jacob, felt that he was not true to his inner self. His behavior reflected an exalted ideal to which he aspired, but which was not authentic. He, therefore, felt awkward and uncomfortable with friends. He longed to be freer with them, to achieve easy comradeship. These needs were stifled by the compulsion to live up to the very high standards for which his family was known. The same dilemma I faced with the first client was present with Jacob. Were psychological factors predominant or was this pride which should be addressed as a moral problem? In this case, the problem was resolved when further sessions revealed unhealthy familial patterns of behavior. My approach was an integrated one, combining dynamic psychotherapy with spiritual counseling. Jacob was anxious and distressed, unsure as to whether to continue his present lifestyle or to alter it. A change would startle family and friends. His present behavior was, in most respects, above reproach, extreme in its repression of anger, even when warranted. It entailed siding with some members of his family who disapproved of other members' habit of denigrating acquaintances. The denigrating behavior was rationalized as not tolerating sham and hypocrisy. Although it was perhaps a bit warranted, its extremity and aggressiveness caused Jacob to be overly gentle.

His inner conflict was discussed. He agonized as to whether to continue following in his illustrious family's footsteps or to carve out for himself, in some areas, a slightly different lifestyle. I related a story of a Hasidic master. The master—Rebbi—was criticized for not following in his father's footsteps regarding modes of prayer, study, etc. He retorted that, on the contrary, he does not deviate from his father's customs; his father did not follow blindly in his father's footsteps and he, as well, does not imitate his father. An additional discussion centered on the specific and unique characteristics of the three patriarchs, insofar as to how they saw fit to serve God. Abraham's uniqueness was in his chesed—the performance of acts of loving-kindness. He understood that chesed was the rationale underlying God's reasons for creating the world. He, therefore, chose to follow in the Almighty's footsteps and to relate to Him in this fashion. His son, Isaac, exemplified "gevurah"—literally strength, meaning strength of will, reflecting the strength, the power with which the Almighty created the universe. Isaac served God by living his life in accordance with the precepts of gevurah which reflects his willingness to be sacrificed. Jacob combined both traits so as to be a mirror of God's glory; he is depicted by the sages as being a living example of Torah. The lesson derived is that within the Torah's parameters, there is ample leeway, within the Halachic framework, to enable individual spirituality to be expressed. This principle is vividly illustrated by the Chofetz Chayim's interpretation of a teaching of the Talmud. It portrays the future, metaphorically, as God sitting in the center of a circle surrounded by the righteous. He noted that the center of a circle is equidistant from all points on its perimeter. This signifies that, although there are diverse ways within Halacha's framework of serving Him, they all are equally favorable in God's eyes.

It was already noted that the legitimization of spiritual counseling paves the way to sometimes include ethical moral guidance as an adjunct of spiritual therapeutic counseling. To further clarify this, it seems necessary to emphasize that just as therapeutic spiritual counseling is not a vehicle to deliberately further religious practice, but aims to integrate psychological principles with spiritual insights to bolster mental health, in similar fashion we can now think in terms of integrating psychotherapy with the knowledge and techniques employed by clergymen and moralists in our endeavors to help the client face his difficulties. Therapy can now be perceived as a richer method, as freer when necessary, to unshackle itself from its previous narrow boundaries and be able to deal with the individual as a whole, not as a fragmented person.

This new perception is not an invitation to parents, clergymen, and teachers to abandon their traditional roles as teachers of ethics and morality. Only in cases where therapeutic intervention is called for, due to some measure of emotional pathology, can the therapist also address himself to areas related to ethics and morals. Perhaps this also will change in the future, but even if that occurs, parents, teachers, and rabbis should not abandon their responsibilities. The underlying assumption in this new perception of psychotherapy is that the boundary between psychotherapy and moral guidance is not as solid or impregnable as it was in the past. A note of caution is in order here. Unless therapists have been highly trained in understanding and relating to moral ethical issues, they should not consider themselves by dint of their professional psychological training to be experts in unraveling complex moral ethical problems.

All of the above leads us back to the issue of flawed character traits. The points discussed seem to justify including their treatment as part of psychotherapy under certain circumstances. The addition and inclusion of therapeutic spiritual psychotherapy provides the theoretical and practical bases for this new direction.

The inclusion of moral issues in therapeutic spiritual counseling circumvents an issue raised by Wallach and Wallach.[1] Some psychologists claim that aside from alleviating emotional pain, therapy influences patients to become better, kinder people. Wallach and Wallach present arguments that, on the contrary, many therapeutic systems make people more selfish and self-centered. This position is endorsed by Wicklund and Eckert.[2] They contend that psychotherapy overemphasizes the self to the exclusion of others. They marshal arguments which they believe show that this is diametrically opposed to the Judeo-Christian heritage. Weaving spiritual counseling and addressing ethical issues into the therapeutic process counteract whatever deleterious influence therapy may exert. Richards and Bergin's[3] feeling is that getting in touch with one's spiritual core facilitates the dissolving of what they term the "moral overplay," leading to elimination of pathology. This, of course, is an aspect of spiritual therapeutic psychotherapy.

In chapter two, the concept of the unconscious was discussed in connection with the analysis of concepts common to both Judaism and psychotherapy. The discussion centered there primarily on the theoretical aspects of the unconscious. In this chapter, the focus is upon the practical therapeutic aspects of the unconscious. In my therapeutic work, I introduce the concept by presenting it as having been promulgated by the giant Talmudist and saintly personality, Reb Yisroel Salanter (Rabbi Israel Salanter-Lipkin). He related the following hypothetical story. A scholar has an apt student to whom he is strongly attached, and a son, a wastrel whom he despises. All three reside in the same town and are asleep when a fire erupts. The scholar is awakened from a deep sleep and told of the fire sweeping the town. He will instinctively hasten to rescue his son, not his student. This is so because not being yet fully awake, he is not in possession of his rational cognitive faculties. In such a state, the instinctual "inner" forces are dominant and the rational "outer" forces are unable to influence behavior. The concept of inner and outer forces is used by him to explain two apparently contradictory sayings of the sages. In one teaching, Abraham is described as eagerly and joyously obeying God's command to sacrifice his son. In a different teaching, he is depicted as weeping. Reb Yisroel resolves the contradiction by explaining Abraham's behavior as a function of both inner (unconscious) forces and outer (conscious) forces. On the conscious level, he cheerfully prepared to carry out the Almighty's wish, but inner instinctual forces caused his weeping; they could not be denied their measure of grief. Inner unconscious forces, personality components, cannot be eliminated or controlled to the extent that they will not be experienced. Inner forces are "unclear" forces; outer forces are "clear" forces. This distinction explains why inner forces are more powerful than outer forces; they are not familiar and seem to the person to emerge from nowhere and overwhelm the unwary. This phenomenon adds understanding to the importance emphasized in Judaism to self-understanding as discussed in chapter two.[4]

With Hasidic clients, it is useful to introduce the concept of the unconscious by relating it to sayings of Hasidic masters. Note #19 of chapter two is a fine example. Presented here are additional sources.

The "Chidushai Horim," the founder of the dynasty of Hasidut Gur, comments on Sinai and the golden calf.[5] He states that, despite the obviously high spiritual level that the Israelites achieved when they entered the covenant with God enthusiastically declaring "Na'aseh Venishma"—we will observe the law and listen to the Almighty's wishes, something was lacking. The enormous devotion they showed, dedicating themselves to following Him without previously ascertaining what was required of them, was nevertheless deficient. The Rim writes that this trumpet call was somewhat lacking in authenticity. Claiming a high spiritual level which was not the true measure of their devotion is an act lacking total spiritual honesty. This revolutionary perception of the Rim is to be understood as referring to the unconscious level. On a conscious level, they were fully committed to their proclamation; indeed this act merited enormous praise. The slight blemish on the unconscious level planted the roots which led he feels, in a short while, to adoration of the golden calf. Two of Rabbi Salanter's sayings crystallize this concept. "A person lives with himself for seventy years; nevertheless he doesn't really know and understand himself." He also said: "The gulf separating one's knowledge from one's actions is as wide as that separating the actions and knowledge of two separate people."

The Rim's grandson, the Sefas Emes, was also cognizant and familiar with the concept of the unconscious, although he does not label it as such. He speaks of the thoughts a person has of which he is not aware, using this concept to explain Joshua's behavior. The sages criticize him for waging unnecessarily prolonged wars when conquering Canaan. They attribute this to Joshua's realization that the cessation of the wars liberating Canaan would mean that his own demise was imminent, for in that case his mission was accomplished. The Sefas Emes stresses that prolonging the war was not done consciously. However, on the unconscious level, this seemed to have influenced him. This led to the postponement of the liberation of Canaan.[6]

These concepts and insights were used in the therapy of a young Hasidic student. He was referred because of obsessive compulsive thoughts and the resultant downward spiral in Torah study and prayer. After a few sessions, he voiced his doubts as to the truth of his religious beliefs. He didn't waver in his belief in God, but he was unsure of the principle that Torah is divine. Experienced therapists will not let themselves become engaged in a philosophical discourse, certainly not in a debate which can be interpreted as foisting the therapist's beliefs on the patient. Most therapists would consider the issue as beyond their expertise as psychotherapists. Some therapists would, perhaps, unconsciously express their satisfaction and urge him to pursue a different lifestyle. The Freudian legacy dictated that therapists should believe that a healthy individual should not feel obligated to practice religion. The contemporary spiritually oriented psychotherapy is to consider this a legitimate issue for discussion. I felt that his religious doubts were symptomatic of his emotional disturbance and I began to explore with the client what in his past and present emotional environment may offer a clue to his quandary. This is exploration of the dynamics of his personality similar to what is done in ordinary psychotherapy. In addition, discussion was centered about certain principles enunciated by eminent scholars as to the relation between personality traits and religious beliefs.[7] Rabbis Ziv and Wasserman argue that faith is and should be self-evident. Agnostic and atheistic sentiments are a result of flawed character traits. People wish to follow their wants and desires and feel free and unfettered. This tendency blinds the person to see what in reality is crystal clear and self-evident. This is similar to bribery which blinds the judge and all people to truth and has the power to distort facts. Similarly, a person bound up in his desires is unable to perceive or comprehend religious truth, so this dialog enabled the patient to redirect his thinking, reframing it to look inwardly. It is easier and less threatening to attribute one's religious questioning to philosophical reasoning than to one's baser inclinations.

Therapists often see clients whose level of religious observance does not seem suitable or fitting. This is manifested by adopting religious customs which are appropriate only for accomplished scholars and those who have honed their religious observance to a high degree. This behavior is definitely out of joint for others. The patient is often engrossed in very strictly observing a selected few mitzvot—commandments, or customs—to the exclusion of other good deeds and Torah study. More extremely, it can be religious behavior which does not consider other people's feelings or infringes upon their rights. The comments and perceptive analysis of the Rim are useful and effective in clarifying for the patient a basic religious truth. Adopting religious behaviors which are not appropriate for the client at his present spiritual level is not advisable and is probably harmful. They constitute mere technical acts and are not authentic religious acts. They can lead to dire consequences of which, not the least, is leading the doer astray into thinking that he is advancing in his religiosity, causing him to be arrogant.

The principle that one's religious honesty is central to Judaic thought is taught by the elder of Slobodka, Rabbi N. Z. Finkel, quoted by and explained by Rabbi Aaron Kotler.[8] The Torah relates that Lot, Abraham's nephew and brother-in-law, was saved by angels when God destroyed Sodom. The sages explain that he merited this because he did not inform on Abraham when the latter told the Egyptians that Sarah was his sister (actually his niece). This explanation is baffling. Why is this act considered as that which saved him, when it seems that other good deeds of Lot seem better suited to explain why he was spared? For example, his extraordinary behavior, his readiness to put his life in danger when strangers arrived in Sodom, and the courage he exhibited are certainly greater deeds than the fact that he did not betray his sister and uncle. Rabbi N. Finkel, the elder of Slobodka, explains and Rabbi A. Kotler presents supporting proof, that Lot's actions were not rooted in his innermost personality. By this is meant that it was modeled, copied from Abraham; it was not, however, integrated in his personality, it was not internalized; it does not reflect his authentic spiritual stature, therefore, it was not sufficiently meritorious to save him from Sodom. This principle, so clearly enunciated by the Rim and the elder of Slobodka, is an all-important key in understanding one's behavior. The therapist, however, must realize that it is not a simple task for the client to realize this. It is fraught with danger and evoking and utilizing it is a complex and sensitive undertaking.

Marital discord is an excellent example of the destructive results of flawed character traits. Let us consider the inability to empathize, to see the others' point of view. This inability prevents the person from even conjecturing that perhaps the spouse may have a valid point, an understandable grievance. This, of course, leads to each one being convinced that the spouse should be the one to initiate reconciliation. This difficulty can be overcome, empathy can be taught. A more serious problem is the power struggle which quite frequently emerges. Much of the rancor, the bitterness present in marital discord is a result of the power struggle. A clinician should discern between a genuine power struggle, where one of the spouses seeks to control and maintain power over the other, and where the person's actions may be a desperate attempt to maintain autonomy, a sense of worth, a basic dignity which in reality is a struggle to not being reduced to a non-entity. The power struggle may be rationalized as ideological or for the children's benefit. The trigger can be almost anything: finances, religiosity, fastidiousness, etc.

The combination of dynamic (or cognitive therapy) with spiritual counseling is suited to deal with situations where a power struggle is taking place. The therapist should by his reactions convey the principle that comments by the clients, such as "this is my feeling" when uttered as a declaration meaning "this is it," is not acceptable. The very essence of a successful marital relationship is the ability to transcend one's feelings to be able to see the other's viewpoint. Feeling is a most important ingredient in any relationship with others and is vital in understanding one's self. However, it cannot be used as a final arbiter in understanding or defining one's relationships, both with others and with one's self. If the therapist is perceived as overly relying on intuitions or gut feelings, the message conveyed is that feelings are the paramount concern and the sole guiding factor guiding behavior. This seems incompatible with Judaism which holds that the other's well-being, including his/her feelings, is as important as one's own. Rationality and emotions are to be balanced; the key to achieving this balance is the ability to see the other person's position with an open mind and to feel what the other is feeling. When we speak of feelings, we use the term empathy; when we discuss viewpoints, we speak of having an open mind. All of the above is the essence of good character traits (middot tovot).

Attaining good character traits is the bedrock of Judaism. Rabbi Chayim Vital was the foremost student of the Ari of Sefad and the disseminator of his Torah. He explained, as did the Gra, that the seeming absence of emphasis in the Torah on good character traits, i.e., the lack of specific commandments (mitzvot) is perhaps paradoxically an indication of their importance. It is so basic that it is the entrance, the door to Torah; consequently, it is not comprehensively taught in the Torah. One cannot begin to approach Torah if one has not acquired good character traits. In Hebrew, this principle is enunciated in the maxim, "Proper breeding is prior to Torah" (Derech Eretz, Kodma LaTorah). The moral ethical lessons derived from the lives of the persons described in the Torah attest to the importance attached to ethics in spite of the fact that there are not many specific commandments instructing us in this area. For example, there is no specific commandment to desist from anger, but the stories of the Torah impress upon us the extraordinary moral blemish attached to anger. The sages never tired of presenting these lessons in their teachings.

It is appropriate at this point to quote the Tosfot Yom Tov on Pirkai Avot, Chapter 5, Mishna 11: The Mishna teaches that there are four categories of people as to their method of dealing with anger. The choicest, the most refined, is the person whose personality is that of one who is slow to anger and quick to forgive, to do away with his anger. The Tosfot Yom Tov notes that the Mishna does not mention one who does not get angry. This is so, he writes, because this seems to be a superhuman trait. This seems to be echoed in the commentary of the Midrash Shmuel who writes that even if one succumbs to anger, but immediately attempts to overcome it, to forgive, in that event the person is considered a Hasid, a saintly person. He adds that a person who is never angry is considered an angel; this trait is found only among angels. It may be that others contest this position. Nevertheless, it can be used in a dialog with a client whose self-image is badly tarnished due to his tendency toward anger.

A quasi-philosophical stance sometimes put forth by clients is relevant to our topic. It is argued that a particular behavior is acceptable because it is natural and, therefore, normal. This position is invoked when sexuality in its diverse forms or expressions of deep anger or jealousy are the issue. This simplistic statement is not justified from a Jewish point of view or, for that matter, from the moral ethical position. The naturalness of an act is not a justification for its use. Judaism teaches that humans are engaged in a constant struggle between the materialistic and spiritual components of personality.

The fact that certain behaviors or feelings seem to flow naturally is not an invitation that they be practiced, that the person should indulge in them. Anger and jealousy may at times be viewed as understandable. This, however, is not to be taken as justifying their expression, especially if done so vehemently. Wisdom, common sense, the ability to see the other person's position should prevail. Job, 11:12, teaches that a person at birth is as wild and untamed as a young donkey. Human nature is to be refined so that its spiritual elements are the dominant factors in personality. The Gra writes, "Something which is good from its inception is good. The appellation very good is reserved for that which was evil and was transformed to good."

It is helpful to steer a client who is devastated by his shortcomings to realize that what is done is over and one's energies should be directed toward the future. In his commentary on Genesis, 4:6, Rabbi Ovadiah Sforno sees this as the Almighty's admonition to Cain. Since a mishap has occurred—the rejection by God of Cain's sacrifice—God tells Cain that it is unwise to dwell on it, since it can be rectified, meaning that future proper sacrifices will be looked upon favorably.

NOTES

1. Wallach, M. A., and Wallach, L. (1983). Psychology's Sanction for Selfishness. San Francisco: W. H. Freeman.

2. Wicklund, R. A., and Eckert, M. (1992). The Self-Knower: A Hero under Control. New York/London: Plenum Press.

3. See Casebook (2004). Note No. 10, Chapter 1. P. 17; and A Spiritual Strategy (1997). Note No. 2, Chapter 1, P. 102. Fuller description in notes #2 and #10, Chapter 1.

4. In addition to the Judaic references cited in Chapter 2, the following sources testifying to the importance of self-knowledge are here noted: (a) Eben Ezra, Exodus 31:18; (b) Maharal of Prague in his introduction to Beer Hagolah; (c) Rabbi Yeruchem Levovitz of Mir, Daas Torah, Numbers, 72-74.

5. Chidushai Horim Al Hatorah (1965). Jerusalem: Nachliel, P. 106.

6. Sefas Emes, Torah, Book of Numbers, Matot.

7. Rabbi S. Z. Ziv, the Elder of Kelm. Chochma Umussar, Part 2, Essay 91. (1964). Jerusalem. Rabbi E. Wasserman, Kovetz Maamorim, Maamar Al Emunah (1963). PP. 11-16. Jerusalem.

8. Mishnat Rebbi Aharon. Al Hatorah (2001). PP. 36-40.

Chapter Five

Meditation: The Judaic View

Spiritual psychotherapy literature discusses a vast number of topics. Although all of these cannot possibly be addressed in this volume, some prominent issues merit attention, one of these being the topic of meditation.

The book edited by Miller[1] entitled "Integrating Spirituality into Treatment" contains a chapter by Marlatt and Kristeller on Mindfulness and Meditation. They present a concise and detailed analysis of various meditative techniques. They write, "Meditation practice is often identified as a relaxation technique. Although this is certainly a legitimate aspect of meditation and one that has made these techniques more easily understood, our primary focus is on meditation as an approach to developing mindfulness, whether at a physical, psychological, or spiritual level." They then explain what is meant by mindfulness: "to be fully mindful in the present moment" is to be aware of the full range of experiences that exist in the here and now... Mindful awareness is based on an attitude of acceptance. Rather than judging one's experiences as good or bad, healthy or sick, worthy or unworthy, mindfulness accepts all personal experiences (e.g., thoughts, emotions, events) as just "what is" in the present moment. Mindful acceptance of difficult thoughts or emotional states often transcends negativity... Perhaps the most significant clinical application of mindfulness is the capacity to adopt an observing self... this observing self is also what connects meditation as part of psychotherapy to behavioral techniques, such as self-monitoring, and to cognitive techniques in which characteristic distorted or dysfunctional thoughts are systematically identified... the aim of mediation therapy is not to change the content of the thought itself, but to alter the client's attitude or relationship to the thought."
... Thinking that "my life is a failure" is accepted as just a thought that occurred in the mind... thoughts are accepted as the natural behavior of the mind, but not as inherently defining the self."

At this point, it seems appropriate to present the Jewish stance. True, thoughts do not inherently define the self, but not for the reason given. Thoughts stem from diverse components of personality. As was already noted, Judaism views inner conflict as a basic given of the personality makeup as, for example, the conflict between the materialistic and spiritual components. This train of thought rules out considering a thought as the essence of personality. The person has to analyze himself, delving deeply into the recesses of his mind, his emotions, his past, and his aspirations. Only then can he begin to ascertain the roots of a thought. In theological terms, does it mirror his good or evil inclination? This is not an easy task, but it is incumbent upon the person to attempt to fully understand himself. Further on the authors write, "To the extent that spiritual experience is a universal human capacity, meditation has been proposed, and experienced by many, as a way to cultivate a sense of inner calm, harmony, and transcendence often associated with spiritual growth. Meditation may accomplish this by providing a technique that 'turns off' or 'bypasses' cognitive processing of usual daily preoccupations and concerns, allowing access to these other aspects of living."

The authors describe various types of meditation. Since my purpose is a theoretical analysis in terms of Judaic thought, and not a compendium of techniques, I will be content to refer the interested reader to the chapter by Marlatt and Kristeller. Nevertheless, I will mention two relevant pieces of information. In Richards and Bergin's handbook,[2] there is a chapter by Finn and Rubin entitled "Psychotherapy with Buddhists." They write, "There are two main types of mediation: concentration and insight. In concentrative meditation, one attends without judgment to a specific object such as the breath. It is an exclusive state of mind by which one is absorbed in the particular phenomenon that one is paying attention to. In insight meditation, one is aware of the changing objects of one's experience—sounds, memories, plans, the breath, and so forth."

It is commonly accepted that the roots of meditation are Eastern. However, in her chapter entitled "Crossing Traditions,[3] Cook maintains that Ignatian prayer methods developed by St. Ignatius of Loyola which, in essence, are meditative, are a cornerstone of Catholic spirituality. I feel that it is important to note this, being that what follows is an analysis of a Jewish scholar's thesis that meditation is an ancient Jewish practice.

Meditation has been researched by contemporary scholars, psychologists, medical researchers, and others. Many report that meditation results in decreased anxiety or physiological distress, lowering of heart rates, etc. This research is ongoing and now encompasses the prevention and treatment of addictive behaviors and chronic pain, among other problems.

Neuroscientists as well have begun to interest themselves in the effects of meditation. Their research touches upon the fascinating area of mind-body interaction (see, for example, *Time Magazine*, May 8, 2006). Time lists 100 people whom it considers the world's most influential people. One of those listed is Richard Davidson who is a pioneer in this field. His best-known research is in neuroplasticity. This documents the internal states of consciousness, using Tibetan monks meditating as subjects. His studies show how meditation influences electrical activity in the brain and its effect on consciousness (see also Time Magazine, February 12, 2007, p. 52).

JEWISH MEDITATION

We can now turn our attention to Jewish meditation. Aryeh Kaplan was an American Jewish Talmudist and scholar, a physicist by profession, who wrote widely on Jewish topics. His many books are highly regarded for their lucid presentation of complex areas of Jewish theology. One of his later books, written before he passed away at an untimely age, was "Jewish Meditation."[4]

Rabbi Kaplan contends that meditation has ancient Jewish origins which he presents in some detail. His book is replete with many nuggets of wisdom explaining tenets and rituals related to Judaism's apprehension of Divinity and, as such, are enlightening. A knowledgeable reader can discern from whence Rabbi Kaplan drew his understanding and interpretation of his basic principles of Jewish theology: the classical texts, "Nefesh Hachayim" authored by Rabbi Chayim of Volozhin, the foremost disciple of the Vilnar Gaon (Gra) and Rabbi Shneur Zalman of Lodi in his book "Tanya," the foundation of the school of Lubavitch—Chabad—Chasidus.

My misgivings are directed at his thesis that Jewish theological thought and rituals are rooted in meditative theory and practices. This seems to me an unfounded proposition. I will present my thinking by quoting a number of his arguments and comments and responding to them. I do not quarrel with him as to the fact that it may well be, as he claims, that meditative practices are an adjunct to Jewish spirituality. I do, however, reject the claim that Jewish thought is, to a very large extent, rooted in meditation.

His description of meditation does not basically differ from what was quoted above. He does, however, add the following: "It [meditation] can also involve the most basic of experiences. Suppose, for example, that you are trying to experience the beauty of a rose. Other thoughts intrude obscuring the image of the rose." However, there is another factor that prevents you from experiencing the rose completely. This factor involves spontaneous images that impinge upon the person," a phenomenon he had described earlier. "The reason you are not normally aware of these images is that they are very faint . . . " "No matter how hard you try to focus your mind on the rose, the image of the rose is competing with the self-centered images in the mind . . . In a meditative state . . . it is possible to turn off the interference and concentrate totally on the rose . . . The beauty of the flower when seen in higher states of consciousness is indescribable to someone who has never experienced it . . . This increased awareness can be used in many ways . . . It has been said that one can see the entire universe in a grain of sand."

The author proceeds to describe other uses of the enhanced power of perception engendered in a meditative state. "One of the most powerful uses of meditation is to gain an awareness of the spiritual. Although we may be surrounded by a sea of spirituality, we are not actually aware of it . . . If a person can quiet down all extraneous thoughts he can then 'tune in' to the spiritual. This tuning in is what is known as the mystical experience. In this sense meditation is the most important technique of mystics all over the world."

Rabbi Kaplan embraces mysticism and proceeds to use it in explaining Jewish ritual. Let us examine just a few of his examples.

He writes, "The most vivid experiences were those attained by the prophets in the Bible. In the Biblical sense, a prophet is more than a person who merely sees the future. Rather, he is one who has such a strong experience of the spiritual that he can use it to garner information. Sometimes this information included knowledge of the future, hence the popular conception of a prophet as one who sees what has not yet occurred. Nevertheless, the true prophet has access to many other truths besides knowledge of the future. It is important to realize the important role that meditation played in the careers of the prophets of Israel. On its highest level, meditation can provide a person with an experience of God . . . Our perception of God is often clouded by ego and anthropomorphism, so that we tend to see God as a mirror image of ourselves. By freeing the mind of these encumbrances, meditation can help us to open our minds totally to the experience of God.[5]

Kaplan's description of a prophet and his role is correct. However, the statement that meditation played an important role in prophecy seems unfounded. Many Talmudic scholars relate to prophecy in their writings. In particular, the Rambam (Maimonides) and the Ramchal (Rabbi Moshe Chayim Luzatto) are considered authoritative.[6] Nowhere is it mentioned in either of their works that meditation is a prerequisite in attaining prophecy. For example, in his book "Derech Hashem," part 3 from chapter two onward, the Ramchal delineates the uniqueness of prophecy and the prophet, and does not mention meditation. The prophet had to study a number of things, first and foremost a thorough knowledge of Torah placing him as a leading scholar of his era. He required a teacher to guide him in how to attain spirituality in the sense of holiness and purity. Attaining prophecy required great wisdom and purity of body and soul, the ability to rise above the banal and mundane.

Having reached this spiritual height, the person may or may not be granted the gift of prophecy. It is a gift given by the Almighty.[7] The Torah relates that it was given to Baalam who was not a holy person for reasons known to God.[8] Baalam then wished to curse the Israelites, but was prevented by the Almighty.

Kaplan devotes many pages as to how one can perfect the technique of meditation. He concludes, "When a person becomes expert in visualization [a technique he described] he will be able to see things in the mind's eye that he could never see with his physical eyes. From descriptions in Kabbalistic and other mystical works, it appears that many experiences encountered in higher states of consciousness fall into this category. Thus, for example, the Zohar [a mystical Midrashic work authored by the great tannaic sage, one of the most important scholars mentioned in the Mishna, Rabbi Shimon Ben Yochai] speaks of the 'lamp of darkness.' This appears to denote a darkness that radiates. Similarly, in Talmudic sources, there are references to 'black fire.' There is a teaching that primeval Torah was originally written with 'black fire on white fire.' This is something we cannot see with ordinary vision, and indeed, it is impossible to imagine in a normal state of consciousness. Ordinarily, we see bright colors, not blackness or darkness as radiant.[9] He writes in great detail, purporting to explain the significance of this and other examples.

I am not knowledgeable in Kabbalah, but his arguments in the text seem far-fetched interpretations of his basic thesis. My approach and comments will be better understood if, at first, I will present what I believe is the correct understanding of how Judaic thought relates to the concept of apprehension of the Divine.

Rabbi Meir Simcha (one of the foremost Talmudists and saints of the late 19th and early 20th centuries) in at least two places [Meshech Hachochma, Genesis, 12:7 and Deuteronomy, 11:14] states that the soul possesses a faculty for perceiving the Divine. This is embedded in the human mind as is other, a-priori knowledge, as for example, the concept that the whole is greater than any of its parts. Judaism regards the soul as a spiritual segment of the Divine. Accepting this must invariably lead to the position that the soul can apprehend Divinity.

In his commentary on the Bible {Leviticus, 18:29), the Ramban (Nachmanides) states that the soul is eternal. This, he says, explains why the Torah does not specifically mention that the reward for following the proper path is eternal life. The Ramban says that this is the normal state of affairs; therefore, there is no need to specify this. The Creator breathed into his [man's] nostrils the breath of life (Genesis, 2:7). The Torah does, however, have to teach us that if man sins, God will alter the normal state and cut off the soul from its source.

The concept that the soul is a spiritual segment of the Almighty is articulated by a number of Talmudic scholars. Rabbi Chayim of Volozhin discusses this in "Nefesh Hachayim" (Gate 1, chapters 4-7 and chapter 15; Gate 2, chapter 14). Rabbi Shneur Zalman (Tanya, Chapters 2, 35, and 46) discusses this at length. These spiritual giants and others as well develop the theme that the soul is capable of apprehending Divinity as a function of its own divine nature. Rabbi Chayim Vital, the foremost disciple of the "Ari" and the disseminator of his Kabbalah doctrine, sees in the divinity of the soul the basis of prophecy (Sha'arai Kedusha, Part 3, Gates 3-8). The famed Chazon Ish also relates to this concept in his Chazon Ish, Taharot, Emuna U'bitochon, Chapter 1:9. See also Rabbi A. Y. Kook, Adar Hayokar, p. 30, Mussar Ovicha, p. 98. What may seem more amazing is the sages teaching that the divine soul in its embryonic stage is taught Torah. We are taught that (a) the soul can apprehend divinity and (b) it has imprinted on it cognitive knowledge—Torah (Rabbi Avraham Achi Hagra. Ma'alot Hatorah, pp. 221-223. Jersualem: Keter Torah).

Perceiving the soul as described above as a segment of the Divine obviates the necessity to seek concepts, such as meditation, to explain the high level of spirituality reached throughout the centuries by countless Jewish scholars and saints.

Rabbi Kaplan, as noted above, goes to great lengths (a) to show that meditation played a prominent role in Jewish thought and spirituality and (b) to account for the lack of relating to the concept in Jewish scholarly literature, for the dearth of discussion and analysis of meditative techniques. I am referring to the classic texts which, to this day, are acknowledged as those representing authentic Jewish thought. Kaplan feels that meditation played a key role among Jewish mystics and Kabbalists. However, he is aware, and I quote: "Techniques were alluded to, but always in veiled hints" (p. 46). On the following page, he goes even further. "Soon after Abulafia's time, an event was to occur that would eclipse meditation as the focus of Kabbalah. This was the publication of the Zohar in the 1290s. Although this mystical work contains many allusions to meditative methods, it does not speak explicitly about meditation." His explanation as to why the dissemination of the Zohar eclipsed meditation is that the Zohar is so complex "that it takes a lifetime to understand them (referring to the spiritual systems described in the Zohar). Therefore, he concludes, "Kabbalists now had a new goal, namely, to understand the Zohar" (p. 47). Rather amazingly, he writes: "This made Kabbalah into an academic discipline as well as a mystical one. One begins to find more and more books published on Kabbalah that regard it as a philosophy rather than as an experience." Even the legacy of the Ari, he claims, served to further intellectualize Kabbalah. These statements run counter to the approach and beliefs of the great Jewish thinkers of the past few centuries. On the basis of this and other arguments, Kaplan seems to be viewing the spiritual movements of past centuries differently than how they are generally perceived.

His understanding of the relation between the Hassidic movement and meditation is interesting. He claims that the Baal Shem Tov reintroduced meditation to Judaism. However, for various reasons, Hasidism abandoned this meditative trend and forged new different paths (see pp. 48 and 49). In just a few pages, Kaplan seems to interpret the Hasidic movement differently from how Hasidim and their masters perceive it. This is mere speculation; one does not find another thinker who voiced similar ideas.

On page 46, Kaplan refers to "Sefer Yetziroh" (the Book of Creation) which he believes was published during the Talmudic period. He calls it the most enigmatic text on Jewish mysticism. He informs us that over a hundred commentaries have been proposed to unravel its mysteries, "but they all tend to read their own systems into the text rather than extract its message. Careful analysis of the text, however, shows it to be an extremely advanced text on meditation." The vast majority of those commentators, if not all, are renowned scholars, rabbis who were among the spiritual leaders of their respective generations. Does it seem reasonable that they all erred and that Rabbi Kaplan was privileged to fathom its secret?

In similar fashion, he interprets a saying of the Talmudic sages as fostering meditation. He writes (p. 57), "The Talmud speaks of reviewing a "Mishna" and says, 'Repeating one's mishna one hundred times is not the same as repeating it one hundred and one times.' There may be an allusion in this teaching that even in Talmudic times, the Mishna was used as a type of mantra." There has never been any question in the myriads of commentators who very frequently quote this saying as to its clear and straightforward intent. It is an example of the enormous respect our sages had for studying Torah. Although it would seem that the benefit gained from studying a mishna an additional time, once more, after studying it one hundred times, is negligible; nevertheless, one who does so is extolled and presented as spiritually on a much higher plane than one who is satisfied with his reviewing it one hundred times. Transforming this beautiful lesson into an argument for meditation seems even more than a misinterpretation; regretfully, one must say it is twisting it into something foreign to the spirit of Judaism.

Kaplan postulates that the Menorah (candelabrum) in the Beit Hamikdash (Temple) may have also been viewed as an object of contemplation (p. 69). This startling idea is presented without an iota of evidence, not citing even one relevant teaching of the sages. Needless to say, this is not how Judaic scholars throughout the ages approached the study of Jewish theology.

In chapter 5 of his book, Kaplan presents a detailed complex picture of what he terms the common practice of meditation among the Jews during the closing era of prophecy. He states (p. 42) that during the period when the Bible was written (until approximately 400 BCE), meditation was practiced by a large proportion of the Jewish people. "Regular schools of meditation existed, led by master prophets . . . these meditative schools required a strong discipline and faithful adherence to a strict regimen." He then notes what was required of the students. "A person had to be not only spiritually advanced, but in complete control of all his emotions and feelings. Beyond that, the disciplines of the Torah and commandments were central to these schools . . . It appears that this was one of the attractions of ancient idolatry . . . many idolatrous schools of mysticism and meditation were open to all. A person could at least think that he was having a transcendental experience, without adhering to the tight discipline of Torah and Judaism . . . For many people, it was an experience after which they would actually lust . . . If they could not get it from Israelite sources, they would seek it in idolatrous rites."[10] His thesis is that when the Jews were exiled, the leaders reasoned that, under the new circumstances, danger existed that the masses would be misled and stray from Judaism if meditation would be open to all. Therefore, around this time, the more advanced forms of meditation were hidden from the masses and made part of a secret teaching.

"One of the last great prophets was Ezekiel, who lived in Babylonia right at the beginning of the Exile. The first chapter of the Book of Ezekiel is one of the most mysterious parts of the entire Bible. In it, the prophet describes his visions of angels and the Divine throne in extraordinary detail. According to one tradition, this vision contained the keys to prophetic meditation and, if understood, could serve as a guide to attaining prophecy. The study of this chapter became known as the 'discipline of the chariot' (maaseh merkavah)." The methodology was there, but without the key it could not be understood.

"By the time of the rebuilding of the Second Temple and the establishment of the Second Commonwealth, the Jewish leadership was clearly aware of the dangers that chariot meditation posed if it were made available to the masses." He then notes the dangers and difficulties which could possibly occur if meditation was not curtailed. He writes, "Therefore, the Jewish leadership made a very difficult decision. The benefits of having the masses involved in the highest types of meditation were weighed against the dangers . . . Henceforth, the discipline of the chariot had to be made into a secret doctrine, taught only to the most select individuals . . . The Great Assembly also realized that the general populace would need a meditative discipline . . . The meditative discipline that was composed by the Great Assembly ended up as the Amidah, a standing prayer consisting of 18 sections, which would be repeated silently, in an upright position, three times a day. It is true that nowadays the Amidah is thought of more as a prayer than a meditative device . . . The Amidah was meant to be repeated three times every day from childhood on, and essentially the same formula would be said for an entire lifetime. The Amidah could therefore be looked upon as one long mantra . . . " He concludes, "But most important, there is ample evidence that it was originally composed as a common form of meditation to be used by the entire Jewish nation" (p. 45). However, Rabbi Kaplan does not produce evidence supporting his thesis. He does quote Talmudic sayings informing us that some of the outstanding sages, such as Rabban Yochanan Ben Zakai and Rabbi Akiva, engaged in what he believes are meditative experiences. He, of course, is referring to what is commonly accepted that they were privy to the Torat Hanistar—what we today call Kabbalah, meaning the esoteric and hidden meanings and interpretations of Torah. No Talmudic authority refers to their actions as meditation. In similar fashion, the vision of the prophet Ezekiel is viewed as an integral part of Kabbalah, fully understood only by highly spiritual people who immerse themselves into Kabbalah. However, his contention (p. 44) that the basis for this secretive approach is rooted in meditation is unfounded, not being mentioned in any of the classical texts defining Judaism.

What is perhaps even more amazing is his proposition that to somehow compensate the masses for shunting aside the more advanced forms of meditation, the Great Assembly instituted the prayer of the Amidah (Shemona Esrai) which he views as a meditative device (p. 45). It is stretching the limits of unfettered speculation much too much to see the Amidah, the backbone of the Jewish prayer book, as a meditative device. Prayer is prayer, the turning of the individual to his Creator, the Almighty, acknowledging His kingship, supplicating and thanking Him. The Talmud devotes pages to prayer examining its roots and its nuances. The Talmud (Berochot, 26:B) discusses whether the roots of prayer stem from the three Patriarchs or whether they are in lieu of the sacrifices offered in the Beit Hamikdash (Temple). Referring to the Amidah as one long mantra is patently erroneous.

The spirituality achieved in and by prayer is dependent upon the "kavanah" of the individual who utters the words—the prayer. In rabbinic literature, this is taken to mean concentration—greater kavanah is more intense concentration. Our sages teach us that kavanah is to be understood as signifying that (a) the supplicant is aware that his prayers are directed toward the Almighty, that He alone can grant his wishes; in the words of our sages, he knows he is standing "before God"; and (b) the prayers are recited meaningfully; the one who prays knows their meaning and directs his mind and heart to uttering them with understanding and feeling. Rabbi Kaplan, however (pp. 49-50), translates kavanah as "directed consciousness" which then leads him to write that it denotes meditation. This, of course, is in keeping with his tendency to place ritual into the cubicle of meditation.

A final example of Kaplan's tendency to insert meditative underpinnings into basic Jewish theological principles is now presented. This example does not finalize the list, but I believe it suffices. He reaches the conclusion that the "self" of humans is "nothingness" (p. 88). When a person uses meditative techniques, he is in touch with the Divine in himself to some degree. In truth, his clarification of this concept is innovative and has merit. Nevertheless, extending the concept of nothingness and identifying it with the self are unwarranted. It stems from his utmost obsessive tendency to see meditation peering from every nook and cranny of Jewish theology and ritual. The Gra (Rabbi Eliyhu of Vilna) has taught us what the self is. He identifies it with the "ruach," which can be translated as the spirit in people. We are taught that the components of humans basically consist of three parts: (a) the "neshama" (soul) which, as noted previously, is a segment of the Divine. It is implanted in humans to guide and elevate them; (b) the "ruach" (spirit) is also in a sense a Divine segment. It is that part of us which is given the task of choice—good or the opposite. It is that part of us which exercises free will and will be held accountable for our actions. (c) The "nefesh" is that part of spirituality that is attached to the body. The Gra holds that the ruach is the self, the neshama is divine, and the nefesh is bodily attached. The uniqueness of each of us is the ruach.[11]

NOTES

1. Miller, William R. (1999). Integrating Spirituality into Treatment. Washington, DC: American Psychological Association. Chapter 4.

2. Richards, P. Scott and Bergin, Allan E. (2000). Handbook of Psychotherapy and Religious Diversity. Washington, DC: American Psychological Association. PP. 324-325.

3. Casebook for a Spiritual Strategy in Counseling and Psychotherapy. Ed. P. Scott Richards and Allan E. Bergin (2004). Washington, DC: American Psychological Association. Chapter 10, P. 177.

4. Kaplan, Aryeh (1985). Jewish Meditation. New York: Schocken Books.

5. Ibid, PP. 9-14.

6. I chose these two spiritual giants for the following reasons. The Rambam's Halachic prominence is unquestioned. He was also the leading Jewish rationalist philosopher. His influence on Judaism and Judaic thought is inestimable. The Ramchal was arguably the leading Kabbalist of his generation. He also authored what is perhaps the most influential book on Jewish ethics, "Mesilat Yesharim."

7. The Talmud Sanhedrin 39:B discusses the relation between the prophet Ovadia and King Achav of Israel. Ovadia was in charge of the king's household. He is described as very God fearing. The Talmud then explains why—for what good deed—he was granted prophecy. The reason given is because he hid 100 prophets in two caves enabling their escape from Izevel's (Isabel's) clutches. This teaches us that being granted prophecy is a gift which is earned through the performance of good deeds. The prophet Jeremiah, however, was chosen, according to Chapter 1, verse 5, before he was born.

8. The sages explained that the Almighty desired that Israel be blessed by a non-Jewish prophet. They also taught that God granted prophecy to a gentile so as to pacify the gentiles who might have complained that they were not granted this gift.

9. Rabbi Kaplan, pages 31 and onward, elaborates on this concept, citing what he believes to be Biblical passages which support his contention.

10. Kaplan's explanation of the attraction idolatry had for Jews ignores the explanation given by the sages (Sanhedrin 64:A). The men of the Great Assembly beseeched God to allow them to eradicate the lust (yetzer harah) that entices Jews to worship false gods. There was a specific evil inclination enticing Jews to worship idols.

11. Orot Hagra (1986). Ed. Y. D. Rubin. Bnai Brak. Kollel Tel Ganim, P. 198.

Chapter Six

Forgiveness: Critique of the "Sunflower"

Forgiveness is one of the methods used in spiritual psychotherapy which is rapidly gaining in importance and is considered one of the most effective tools in its arsenal. This chapter describes it and discusses the Judaic approach.

Richards and Bergin[1] view the relation between repentance and forgiveness thusly, "Repentance can be viewed as a prelude to forgiveness; that is in repentance, people seek forgiveness from God or from those whom they have hurt or offended, and it includes reforming thought, feeling and action. . . . All the theistic world religions teach that people should forgive those who have harmed or offended them and seek forgiveness for wrong doings." They proceed to point out that religions differ in the specifics of forgiveness. "For example, within the Christian tradition, believers are told to forgive 'all enemies and offenders in an unqualified way.' In the Jewish tradition, it may not be viewed as desirable to 'forgive people who do not acknowledge the injury, or even worse, rationalize their injurious behavior as having been deserved.' In some religious traditions (e.g., Catholic, Mormon), confession to church authorities is viewed as a necessary step in seeking forgiveness, whereas in other traditions, confession to religious authorities is not viewed as necessary." We will return later to the issue of how Judaism perceives forgiveness. They write that forgiveness is an act that has important spiritual consequences. However, "forgiveness is an intervention that can be used without any reference to religious or spiritual concepts." They quote research that encouraging forgiveness is one of the most frequently used psychotherapeutic spiritual interventions and that the therapist's religious beliefs were either weakly or completely unrelated to their attitudes about the importance of forgiveness in therapy. They do, however, believe that its effectiveness may be enhanced by tying it to the client's deeply held beliefs.

Sanderson and Linehan[2] also address themselves to the differences between Judaism and other religious traditions: "In Judaism, a man or woman does not ask God to forgive a transgression against another person, nor does he or she grant forgiveness on behalf of others except at the request of others." The latter part is correct; the first part, however, touches upon a more complicated situation. The statement is true insofar as it relates to a transgression committed by the person himself to another. In this instance, she or he cannot beseech the Almighty to forgive before being granted forgiveness by the injured person. After that is granted, the sinner can and should ask God to eradicate, to cleanse him/her, from the sin. By this is meant that, aside from the transgression against the person, the offender has also sinned against the Almighty who does not countenance hurt or injury by one person to another. There is yet another aspect to be considered. The Siddur—the prayer book—is replete with prayers beseeching the Almighty to forgive Israel's transgressions. This is rooted in a basic Jewish theological principle. People are responsible for one another. Prophets were dispatched to inform and teach other nations as was Jonah who was sent to and prophesized in Nineveh. Isaiah lamented the coming destruction of Moab (Isaiah, Chapters 15-16).

Sanderson and Linehan continue, "Only the injured person can grant forgiveness. The Holocaust provides six million examples of this principle . . . In a well-known example of the problem of forgiveness, Simon Wiesenthal, an inmate in a death camp, was asked by an SS guard to grant absolution at the time of the guard's death. Wiesenthal refused, in keeping with Jewish tradition, but he remained haunted by his response. In *The Sunflower: On the Possibilities and Limits of Forgiveness*, Wiesenthal (1998) later surveyed 53 men and women—religious scholars, philosophers, writers, and political figures—on the question of whether he should have forgiven the soldier. Several Christian and Buddhist writers responded with "I believe one should forgive the person or persons who have committed atrocities against oneself and mankind . . . The Jewish writers, in stark contrast, are consistent in their argument that it was not in Wiesenthal's power to forgive." They conclude, "The clinician attempting to help a client struggle with seeking or granting forgiveness must understand the spiritual context of the offended and the offender." In similar fashion, Richards and Bergin[3] write, "We have found that some clients, because of feelings of religious obligation, have attempted to forgive those who have offended them prematurely. Some devoutly religious clients we have worked with have said they felt unworthy and unrighteous because they were not able to forgive others more quickly. We have found it helpful to teach such clients that forgiveness involves a process of reconciliation that often takes considerable time and may require real or imagined encounters with the perpetrators of their pain. With such clients we have found that reframing the client's dilemma in the following manner sometimes has been helpful: 'It isn't that you haven't forgiven your [parents], it's just that you are still involved in the process of forgiving. You are part way through the process, and hopefully our work together will help you eventually complete the process. In the meantime, it appears that you still have a lot of hurt, grief, and anger that you need to talk about and work through. Therapists also should be careful not to encourage clients to seek forgiveness before they have truly taken responsibility for their behavior and done all they can to make restitution for their wrongdoings . . . Even worse, the victim of the wrongdoer may be further harmed by premature or insincere solicitations of forgiveness." We will encounter such a sentiment later on in our analysis of a respondent's answer to the question asked in *The Sunflower*.

Sanderson and Linehan also emphasize the "day-to-day, sometimes grudgingly slow nature of any spiritual practice. Forgiveness, like acceptance, is not a state of grace that one achieves. It is a skill; it is a capacity; it is a practice. Each person may be born with the potential to forgive, but even great spiritual teachers must hone their ability to forgive, particularly when they face great duress." They then present examples of whom they consider spiritual teachers. "It is interesting that all religious traditions offer similar practical instructions for forgiveness. The offender, regardless of his or her belief system, must accomplish five steps: (a) personal responsibility must be acknowledged; (b) sincere regret must be expressed; (c) suitable reparation must be made if possible; (d) a promise must be made to stop the offending behavior; (e) forgiveness must be requested."

Other theorists and clinicians express the same thoughts. Thurston[4] writes, "Perhaps the most powerful (and yet most often misused) spiritual intervention used by therapists with Evangelical and Fundamentalist Christians is that of forgiveness. When done properly, it results in tremendous feelings of freedom, reclaimed personal power, and integrity for the client, as well as in significant spiritual and psychological growth. However, too often, these clients are exhorted by their church to forgive others in a way that denies the extent of their injury, and which both forecloses and short-circuits vital steps in the process, which leads to powerlessness and a lack of internal integration in the client . . . only when the client reaches a place where the client feels more powerful than the offender will it be possible for him or her to forgive that person, while retaining a healthy sense of self."

Sanderson and Linehan report that clinical and counseling psychologists extended forgiveness to include "letting go of anger at oneself over limitations, imperfections and errors." Others as well echo this refrain. Dobbins[5] writes that Pentecostal Christians who, in spite of feeling forgiven by God, have difficulty forgiving themselves.

Krejci[6] reports a fascinating account of marital therapy in which the issue of forgiveness played a prominent part. Mary and John "believed that as Christians, they were expected to forgive each other and initially they thought they had forgiven the other. Yet, their forgiveness was short-lived and was entirely a cognitive process. They described numerous instances when they were offended by the actions of the other, had made a conscious decision to 'forgive and forget,' yet when the next transgression occurred the memory and emotions of the previous events came flooding back with accompanying anger." Therapy included specific instruction as to the process of forgiving and led to the following outcome. "Even though Mary and John developed a deepening sense of forgiveness over the later sessions, the process of forgiveness was not linear as they needed to rework several issues. They recognized that forgiveness falls along a continuum and is not a yes or no issue as it is for their God. They also saw God's forgiveness as spiritual, but worked toward recognizing that their own forgiveness had to also be cognitive and emotional."

In the section "the therapist's commentary," Krejci notes what I consider to be an important insight into how some interpret forgiveness. "An issue that needs to be addressed with some couples is the idea that they do not have to forgive. Some Christians believe that because God forgives, they do not have to. Invariably these people turn the forgiveness over to God, but keep harboring their own resentment." This attitude may explain some of the differences toward forgiveness noted earlier between Christians and Jews. It may be that God's forgiveness is so deeply ingrained in some devout Christians that human forgiveness loses some of its potency and does not, therefore, carry the emotional intensity which Jews attribute to it. This, in turn, leads some to regard its granting as a lighter task and, perhaps paradoxically, as a more pressing obligation than as Jews perceive it. I will return to this issue when the book, *The Sunflower*, is discussed.

Other conceptions of clients are recorded by Slife, Mitchell, and Whollery.[7] (1) "Forgiveness means giving someone permission to continue their wrong behavior; (2) Forgiveness is only a verbal statement which cannot be trusted; (3) Forgiveness can only come after forgetting; (4) Forgiveness can only be given when someone deserves to be forgiven." The authors recorded these thoughts of a client written by her in her journal.

At this point, I think it useful to quote similar comments found in the literature on forgiving.[8]

1. Some ask for forgiveness, but add that I would not have done these things if you were not the person who you are. Obviously, this is not taking responsibility for what has transpired.

2. If the client is angry at God, but is hesitant to express it, one therapist told a client God already knows what you are feeling. He will not get angry with you for telling Him how upset you are feeling at Him.

This chapter began with a brief discussion of the relation between repentance and forgiveness. This topic is in need of further elaboration. I have touched upon this in my chapter in *Casebook*[9] entitled "Judaic Therapeutic Spiritual Counseling." That chapter describes a number of therapeutic interventions and case histories where theses interventions were employed. Briefly, teshuva—repentance—is one of the most prominent features of Judaic spiritual counseling. It is intricately tied to the concept of forgiveness. These concepts denote more than a simple erasure of sin. The literal meaning of the Hebrew term teshuva is returning, signifying a return to the Almighty. This return has its counterpart in God's full embrace of the one who returns. The penitent is regarded as closer to Him than one who has not sinned [Maimonides—Rambam. Mishneh Torah. Laws of Repentance, Chapter 7:4]. Teshuva was created before the creation of the cosmos. This startling teaching of the sages indicates the extreme importance of teshuva. It testifies to the love the Almighty has for all humans. They also teach that teshuva cannot be understood rationally. Logic, reason, cannot explain its power, its inherent mechanism which not only eradicates sin, but moves the person even closer to the Almighty. Moreover, if teshuva was initiated and done through all-embracing love of the Creator, the transgression is transfigured to become a meritorious act. God metaphorically bores a hole under His throne to accommodate baalei-teshuva, penitents. David is the archetype and exemplifies the highest degree of repentance to which one can aspire. The three patriarchs, Abraham, Isaac, and Jacob are the base, the foundation upon which Judaism, both as a religion and a nation, is based. They are likened to a stool with three legs. The fourth leg is reserved for David, for teshuva. Note the fact that he is descended from Judah, the fourth son of Jacob, who also exemplified teshuva with his admission of his relationship with Tamar [Genesis, Chapter 38]. The sages teach us that his public admission to this showed that he was the proper choice to lead Israel, to be that from whom the line of kingship proceeds.

Teshuva is a positive commandment. [The Torah is composed of negative prohibitions and positive commandments, together 613 commandments—mitzvot.] It, therefore, is subject to parameters dictated by Jewish law—Halacha. However, even in instances where the penitent does not meet all the Halachic requirements, he/she is nevertheless considered a baal-teshuva penitent.[10] This means that teshuva is a mitzvah which is not an all or nothing endeavor; it is on a continuum. David achieved the highest plane and is therefore worthy of being the prototype of a penitent.

The seemingly irrational basis of teshuva, the erasure of an event, a sin, prompted the exiled Jews after the destruction of Solomon's temple to doubt its acceptability by the Almighty (Ezekiel, Chapter 33). Scripture relates that only God's swearing attesting to its acceptance allayed their doubts. Some clients who may remain unconvinced are referred to their daily prayers. The Amidah, the central prayer recited three times a day, includes a prayer beseeching forgiveness. This prayer turns to the Almighty as one who continually forgives. There is no limit to His forgiveness, as stressed by Rabi Schneur Zalman of Lodi-Lubavitch in his Iggert Hateshuva.

Teshuva is a rich mosaic of ideas and concepts. Rabbi Dr. J. B. Soloveitchik confers upon teshuva the mantle of creation, self-creation.[11] The penitent may be advised to adopt a different new name and move to a different location, thereby signifying that he/she is a different person, not the sinner.

Rabbi Kotler[12] analyzes the significance of Rosh Hashanah, the New Year. He perceives it as a new beginning in a spiritual sense, as well. Rosh Hashanah inaugurates the ten days of repentance culminating in Yom Kippur, the Day of Atonement. The sages point out that the Torah phrases the mitzvah, obligation, to offer sacrifices in the temple on Rosh Hashanah in language differing from that ordinarily used to describe other sacrifices. The language clearly indicates that Rosh Hashanah is a new beginning, even for sinners who have not as yet repented. The psychological value of this realization is that it motivates the person to change. Once this decision is reached, the person can then devote himself to erasing the spiritual moral blemishes, to repent, to be able to usher in Yom Kippur with genuine feelings of remorse and resolutions to act differently in the coming year.

Repentance is the prerequisite for forgiveness. Punishment by the Almighty can be postponed by Him even in the absence of repentance, but forgiveness is dependent upon repentance. Offenses committed by people against other people are also considered sins against the Almighty. His forgiveness follows only after the offender placates the injured party.

I deem it relevant to our discussion to quote from an essay by Simon Robinson in Time Magazine of March 20, 2006. He comments on the resignation of the Rev. Julie Nicholson, an Anglican vicar, of her position as a parish priest. Rev. Nicholson lost her 24-year-old daughter in July's terrorist bombing in London. Nicholson decided that there are some things in life unforgivable by the human spirit. Therefore, she said, "It is very difficult for me to celebrate the Eucharist and lead people in words of peace and reconciliation and forgiveness, when I feel very far from that myself."

The essayist comments, "We used to hear about the power of forgiveness from the pulpit; now we get it as another word for moving on, the constant refrain of daytime talk shows and self-help books. Psychologists believe that forgiveness can heal deep trauma, but the concept has become so commonplace that everybody publicly asks for it, from Bill Clinton (for marital infidelity) to celebrities (for assorted addictions), to third-world countries (for debt).

Robinson continues, "But personally forgiving someone who has killed your loved one is one of the hardest things we can ever do . . . Microwave-oven-forgiveness—where you just pop something in and bing!—that will never last." The following quote is from Piet Meiring, a professor of theology in South Africa. "There must be," says Meiring, "a sense that forgiveness is balanced by Justice." Following this principle, Robinson writes, "Julie Nicholson will never have that opportunity (to see a balance of forgiveness and justice). Part of the perversity of a suicide bombing is that the murderer dies along with the victims. There is no way to enact the justice that is an essential part of true forgiveness." This is a profound comment.

ANALYSIS OF THE SUNFLOWER

The Sunflower[13] was authored by Simon Wiesenthal. Mr. Wiesenthal is renowned as a Holocaust survivor who established a center for tracking down Nazi murderers and hauling them, when possible, before courts of justice. In the book he describes some of his enormous suffering as a Jew under the Nazis. He relates a most unusual experience which left him with a moral dilemma as to whether he acted properly in a situation into which he was thrust. The first part of the book describes the situation in vivid, emotional tones tempered by his rationality, told in what can perhaps be said to be colored by poetic sensitivity amid all the anguish and death which surrounded him. He turned to clergymen, writers, thinkers, and other who suffered from evil regimes, and requested that they voice their opinions as to whether he acted properly. My references are to the revised edition which includes more respondents than in the previous edition. It is an amazing book; to call it thought provoking is an understatement. The experience and his and others' comments and thoughts touch upon every moral and emotional fiber of humans. I feel it important to relate to this book in this volume on *Judaic Spiritual Psychotherapy* because in its pages are discussed many facets of forgiveness. Discussing and analyzing them broadens our perception of the parameters and implications of forgiveness. Perhaps not everything touched upon is directly applicable to clinicians, but I believe it adds depth and meaning to this vastly important topic.

Forgiveness is a therapeutic tool which is exercised by an injured party. The harm discussed in the Wiesenthal experience is of a different magnitude and takes place in the most extenuating circumstances possible, thus differing immensely from the usual therapeutic situation. Nevertheless, its intellectual and emotional insights can be of use to clinicians practicing therapy. To this end, the following pages are presented and I ask the reader's indulgence in following my ruminations as they may seem to be only tangential to our subject matter.

Simon Wiesenthal was a prisoner of the SS assigned to a work team. He describes the enormous physical hardships, humiliations, constant dread and fear for his life, leading at times to an almost fatalistic approach to his and his fellow prisoners' existence. The prisoners never knew when a group of SS soldiers or other sadistic guards would suddenly pounce upon them and subject them to sadistic torture. Frequently they would turn vicious dogs upon them resulting in death or horrible mutilation. On one occasion, when they reached their work destination, he was approached by a nurse and asked to accompany her. He was led, strangely enough, to the technical school which he had attended. In this school he and other Jewish students were often subjected to beatings by other anti-Semitic students who were supported by some anti-Jewish professors. He was led into a room where a bed stood which was occupied by a person swathed in bandages. Simon was told that he was brought because he's Jewish, by the request of the bed-ridden person. That person was a wounded, blind, dying SS soldier. This soldier had been wounded in a battle on the Russian front and asked for a Jew, whom he hoped would grant him forgiveness for atrocities which he and his fellow SS soldiers committed against Jews.

The narrative is gripping. The soldier talks about himself, the only son of a devout Catholic family. He was the favorite of the parish priest. His father was a staunch anti-Nazi. The boy joined the Hitler youth and later, voluntarily, the SS. This caused an estrangement between son and father for the rest of their lives. The horrendous acts described by the soldier and for which in particular he asked forgiveness from Simon, the Jew, are as follows. Their contingent of SS soldiers rounded up the Jews of a town, approximately 250 people, mostly women, young children, and the elderly. They were all packed into a small house and ordered to carry cans of petrol into the building. A machine gun was posted outside and the soldiers readied themselves. They then threw hand grenades into the building, igniting it. Karl, the soldier, goes on to describe a father holding his young son, shielding the boy's eyes, and jumping from a window. They were promptly shot. The soldier asks for forgiveness from Simon whom he feels can do so in the name of the murdered people. Simon did not grant his wish; on the other hand, he did not leave, although he wished he had, because Karl asked him to remain. He also held Karl's hand when requested by Karl and chased away a bothersome fly which was annoying the solder.

Simon discussed the incident with his fellow prisoners, two Jews and later on with a Catholic who had been a seminary student preparing for the priesthood. Simon was not at peace with himself, wondering whether his silence was justified. After the war, he sent the manuscript of *The Sunflower* to others, as noted above, soliciting their opinions as to whether he should have "forgiven." Interestingly, the SS soldier bequeathed to him his few belongings which Simon refused to accept.

After the war, Simon visited the dead soldier's mother who lived with the thought that Karl had been a good person. The father had already died, never reconciling himself to the fact that his son had been a Nazi. Simon did not reveal the truth, preferring to let the mother continue thinking that her son had been a decent human being.

The views expressed by the respondents differ from one another in the wide range of opinions expressed, the emotions articulated, and the philosophical approaches presented. They also differ in what seems to me the depth of their thoughts and the empathy and sensitivity shown to the unique situation in which Simon was. Some who also suffered under totalitarian regimes seemed fastened on their experiences and in some instances, so it seems to me, failed to appreciate the supremely unique situation in which Simon and others Jews found themselves. Others inserted other issues aside from the central issue of forgiveness. Some comments were philosophical; others, a small minority, were phrased in words bordering on the poetic. I was amazed by the high quality of analytical reasoning of some and sorely disappointed by, what seems to me, rather superficial reasoning of others.

Sanderson and Linehart, who were quoted above in the book edited by Miller, point out that Jewish respondents uniformly held that Wiesenthal acted correctly, whereas Christians and Buddhists generally leaned toward forgiveness. The reason given for the Jewish stand is, " . . . are consistent in their argument that it was not in Wiesenthal's power to forgive." In Judaism, as previously noted, a person cannot forgive on behalf of others; only the injured person can grant forgiveness. This principle is correct from a Judaic point of view. However, their assertion that one cannot petition God to forgive a transgression committed against another person is not entirely accurate. Abraham pleaded with the Almighty to forgive the sins of Sodom. The sages teach that the Sodomites' primary sins were those directed against others. True, Abraham's prayer was couched in terms of forgiving the city on behalf of the righteous, if there be any; nevertheless, one sees that under certain circumstances one can petition the Almighty to forgive others.

One respondent, whose comments are congruent with Sanderson and Linehart's position that Jewish reactions differ from those of Christians, attempted to ascertain what causes this difference. Prager writes, " . . . have led me to conclude that Christianity and Judaism, or perhaps only Christians and Jews have differing views of evil and what to do about it. He cites an example: Whereas the Soviet communist regime persecuted both Christians and Jews, only Jews felt impelled to organize an outcry which eventually led to relief. He asks, "Why was there no outcry from the world's billion Christians, while the 13 million Jews of the world made Soviet Jewry a household word?"[14] He relates an amazing fact. In 1982, the world's best-known Protestant, the Reverend Billy Graham, went to the Soviet Union. Instead of taking the side of his downtrodden co-religionists, he reportedly took the side of the Soviet authorities. He is quoted as telling the churches that "God gives you the power to be a better worker, a more loyal citizen, because in Romans 13, we are told to obey the authorities."

His analysis cites four reasons for the differing attitudes of Christians and Jews. I will mention two of them. "The Christian doctrine of forgiveness has blunted Christian anger at those who oppose them: the notion that one should pray for one's enemies has been taken to mean pray for them, do not fight them . . . and the Christian emphasis on saving souls for the after-life has led to some de-emphasis on saving bodies for this life."

Not all Christians concurred with the opinion that Simon was empowered to forgive and should have forgiven. No less a personage than a prince of the church, Cardinal Franz Konig, Archbishop of Vienna, wrote, "Your story is shocking, and not only because of the horrors you had to witness as a concentration camp prisoner. I found just as shocking your account of your student days and previous life at the university [technical school] . . . Even though an individual cannot forgive what was done to others, because he is not competent to do that, there is still a question of whether one may forgive. The distinction between whether we can forgive and whether we may forgive still leaves unresolved the question of whether we should forgive. You did the dying man a great service by listening to him despite your internal reluctance, by showing him sympathy, by giving him an opportunity to confess his crimes and express his regret, which means you acknowledged his inner conversion . . . Even though you went away without formally uttering a word of forgiveness, the dying man somehow felt accepted by you; otherwise he would not have bequeathed you his personal belongings. Considering your situation at the time and recalling what you went through, an explicit pardon would have surpassed our concept of the human." The Cardinal concludes that had Simon pardoned the soldier, it would have been "an act of almost superhuman goodness in the midst of a subhuman and bestial world of atrocities."

Simon's fellow prisoner, Bolek, a Christian who was studying for the priesthood, at first felt that Simon should have forgiven the SS soldier. However, toward the end of their extended conversation, Bolek faltered in his conviction. "We (Simon and Bolek) talked for a long time, but came to no conclusion. On the contrary, Bolek began to falter in his original opinion that I ought to have forgiven the dying man, and for my part I became less and less certain as to whether I had acted rightly."

As noted above, Simon visited the soldier's mother. He did not destroy her illusion that her son had been a "good boy." After his meeting with her, Simon recorded his thoughts. He writes, "Today the world demands that we forgive and forget the heinous crimes committed against us. It urges that we draw a line, and close the account as if nothing had ever happened. We, who suffered in those dreadful days, we who cannot obliterate the hell we endured, are forever being advised to keep silent. Well, I kept silent when a young Nazi, on his deathbed, begged me to be his confessor. And later, when I met his mother, I again kept silent rather than shatter her illusions about her dead son's inherent goodness. And how many bystanders kept silent as they watched Jewish men, women, and children being led to the slaughterhouses of Europe? There are many kinds of silence. Indeed it can be more eloquent than words, and it can be interpreted in many ways . . . The crux of the matter is, of course, the question of forgiveness. Forgetting is something that time alone takes care of, but forgiveness is an act of volition, and only the sufferer is qualified to make the decision."

Eva Fleischner is a Christian and a professor of religion. She was also a member of the Church Relations Committee of the U.S. Holocaust Memorial Council and of the Advisory Board of the U.S. Catholic Conference Office of Catholic-Jewish Relations. She tells us that she used The Sunflower as a text in her Holocaust course which invariably led to animated discussions. "One striking feature of these has been that, almost without exception, the Christian students came out in favor of forgiveness, while the Jewish students felt that Simon did the right thing by not granting the dying man's wish. What is going on here," she asks. In her analysis she comes to the following conclusions. "If this is so, if both traditions believe in a merciful God, if both stress the need for repentance, why the difference in response among my students? I attribute this to two factors. The first is what I believe to be a widespread misunderstanding among Christians of Jesus' teaching of his oft-quoted admonition to his followers in the Sermon on the Mount to 'turn the other cheek' (Matt., 5:39). Jesus is referring here to wrong done to me, and is asking me not to retaliate. He is not saying that, if someone wrongs me, someone else should 'turn the other cheek'; or, if another is wronged, that I should forgive the perpetrator . . . But, I ask again, was it possible for Simon to grant Karl's request? And I answer quite emphatically, no. Only the victims were in a position to forgive; and they are dead, put to death in the most inhuman ways conceivable." Professor Fleischner proceeds in her analysis (pp. 141-143). Her intellectual acuity and sensitivity are indeed noteworthy.

Other Christians as well voiced these sentiments. Matthew was a Roman Catholic priest who later became an Episcopal priest. He writes, "When a Catholic confesses his sins, and the S.S. man was a lapsed Catholic, he not only is to tell the whole story, but also to undergo penance, to demonstrate his sorrow and contrition. It seems to me that in this regard, Simon acted as the ideal confessor. He gave Karl the only penance available to him to bestow: Silence. The penance of Karl's having to be alone with his conscience before he died. Simon did not offer him forgiveness as a Jew—how could he forgive in the name of even one in that home of hundreds who were torched or the millions in camps of death? But Simon, summoned as a priest confessor, let the man speak his heart. Some sins are too big for forgiveness, even for priests . . . This was Simon's compassion, to stay and listen and even to remain silent and refuse to offer cheap forgiveness to so heinous a crime. These are sins that God and not humans must forgive. And no one had anointed Simon to forgive in God's name." He concludes further on, "For there is no compassion without justice. Simon does not condemn the criminals he uncovers; he leaves that up to the judges of the courts." Here Matthew is referring to Simon's life's work of trying to find Nazi criminals and bringing them to trial. He sees Simon's work "to break the silence, to keep alive the fuller truth of what transpired."

An opinion by a prominent priest, the President Emeritus of the University of Notre Dame, is that he (the priest) would have forgiven. "If asked to forgive, by anyone for anything, I would forgive because God would forgive." He bases his feeling on the fact that he is a Catholic priest. "In a sense, I am in the forgiving business." He explains his perception of his role as follows. "If I suffered as so many had, it might be much more difficult, but I hope I would still be forgiving, not from my own small position, but as a surrogate for our almighty and all-forgiving God."

Reverend Hesburgh's opinion and explanation that he perceives himself as a surrogate is, I assume, the official Catholic position as to the role of a priest.

Mary Gordon, a best-selling author and professor at Barnard, perceives a priest's role differently. In her analysis, she attempts to understand the Nazi's frame of mind. "What does the Nazi expect to gain from forgiveness? Perhaps he imagines that forgiveness is a kind of magic eraser, a way of undoing what cannot temporally be undone, a way of saying it never happened. It becomes, then, a narcissistic rather than a moral act because it places the perpetrator's need to be purged of guilt ahead of the victim's need for restitution or simple recognition of having been harmed . . . The Nazi officer is wrong to ask Wiesenthal for forgiveness for two reasons. First, he is wrong to ask one man to serve as a public symbol for all Jews. A symbol, by its nature, is communal and its status can be bestowed only by the community . . . A priest can forgive sins in the name of God, but he is acting outside of his own biography. His role is mediator between the community and God. But it is the community that gives him that role." Her reasoning uncovers an additional facet of the issue. "Simon Wiesenthal cannot be this dying man's confessor. As a private person, and not a priest, he may act only in his own name. No one can grant forgiveness as a private person in the name of another for that would be theft of the wounded person's right to forgive or not to forgive. But one can forgive for another in a ritual context, if that ritual takes place with the authority of the community. And for the ritual to have any meaning, the atonement must match the crime. If the dying Nazi soldier wished to atone, he should have insisted that he be placed in the camps, so that he could die in the miserable circumstances of those in whose name he is asking forgiveness." Similar proposals are advanced by other respondents, as well.

Other Christians, as well, feel that the Nazi had no right to ask forgiveness of Simon. He should have petitioned God. His request smacks of "cheap grace," a position previously noted. Terence Prittice writes, "and I cannot see how it could be other than mock-forgiveness, granted simply because a man happened to be dying. To forgive this one S.S. man would mean, by implication, to forgive every other S.S. man who murdered, on his deathbed."

The narrative and the opinions voiced by the respondents is a virtual treasure of insights which can be mined. One can, of course, agree or disagree with the merits of the arguments and attitudes. In addition, a reader can delve into the different attitudes of, for example, Buddhists as contrasted to those of Christians, Jews, and atheists. Another facet worthy of analysis is the reactions of those who themselves suffered. Are they different from the others? Touching upon the positions of non-Europeans, who historically and emotionally are more removed from the issue than westerners, should prove enlightening. However, to do all of the above is to overstep the boundaries of this book.

Before concluding this section, there are some comments which I feel are in place. In his account to Simon, Karl mentioned that he saw Jews when his unit was stationed in Poland. There, he at times gave the starving Jews food, but stopped when his platoon leader caught him doing so. However, he says, he would then leave food on the table when he knew that the food would be found by the Jews who cleaned the soldiers' quarters. On the other hand, although acknowledging his heinous acts and expressing sorrow for them, he nevertheless said, "Look, those Jews [those who were burned alive in the house] died quickly; they did not suffer as I do—though they were not as guilty as I am." This sentence is grating. In his account, he spoke of parents and a child in the house. The child's clothes were burning and the father, shielding his son's eyes, elected to jump from the burning window. It is difficult to imagine a more horrendous situation.

Joshua Rubenstein writes of Germans who resisted the Nazis and were executed. He relates an amazing story. "There was the extraordinary example of Reinhard Heydrich's younger brother, Heinz, who had been an enthusiastic Nazi [Reinhard was one of the most notorious Nazis whose name will live on in infamy]. But once he grasped the meaning of the final solution (which Reinhard Heydrich had helped design), he forged one hundred passports to help German Jews escape the Reich before committing suicide himself in 1944 in fear that the Gestapo had uncovered his work. Finally, we know of one S.S. officer named Kurt Gerstein who used his access to information to alert the outside world to Hitler's plans to exterminate the Jews." Needless to say, we have not plumbed the depths of this most important issue, teshuva—repentance and forgiveness.

NOTES

1. Richards, P. Scott and Bergin, Allen E. (1997). A Spiritual Strategy for Counseling and Psychotherapy, PP. 211-214. Washington, DC: American Psychological Association.

2. Sanderson, Cynthia and Linehan, Marsha M. (1999). In Integrating Spirituality into Treatment. Ed. William R. Miller. Chapter 10, PP. 199-216. Washington, DC: American Psychological Association.

3. See note 1, P. 213.

4. Thurston, Nancy S. (2000). Psychotherapy with Evangelical and Fundamentalist Protestants. In Handbook of Psychotherapy and Religious Diversity, Ed. P. Scott Richards and Allen E. Bergin. Chapter 6, PP. 131-153. Washington, DC: American Psychological Association.

5. Dobbins, Richard D. (2000). Psychotherapy with Pentecostal Protestants. In Handbook of Psychotherapy and Religious Diversity, Ed. P. Scott Richards and Allen E. Bergin. Chapter 7, PP. 155-184. Washington, DC: American Psychological Association.

6. Krejci, Mark J. (2004). Forgiveness in Marital Therapy. In Casebook for a Spiritual Strategy in Counseling and Psychotherapy. Ed. P. Scott Richards and Allen E. Bergin. Chapter 5, PP. 87-102. Washington, DC: American Psychological Association.

7. Slife, Brent D., Mitchell L. Jay, and Whollery, Matthew (2004). A Theistic Approach to Therapeutic Community: Non-Naturalism and the Alldredge Academy. In Casebook for a Spiritual Strategy in Counseling and Psychotherapy. Ed. P. Scott

Richards and Allen E. Bergin. Chapter 5, PP. 35-54. Washington, DC: American Psychological Association.

8. Comments found in Casebook, note no. 6, P. 96, and Handbook, note no. 4, P. 146.

9. Note no. 6, Chapter 7, PP. 119-140.

10. Mabit. Bait Elokim. The Mabit was one of the leading Talmudists of the 16th century. He resided in Sfad, northern Israel, and wrote, among other books, Bait Elokim: House of God.

11. Soloveitchik, Joseph B. (1983). Halakhic Man. Philadelphia: Jewish Publication Society of America. P. 110.

12. Kotler, Aaron (1998). Mishnat Rebbi Aharon. Vol. 2, P. 193. Lakewood, NJ: Mochon Mishnat Rebbi Aharon.

13. Wiesenthal, Simon (1969, 1998). The Sunflower: On the Possibilities and Limits of Forgiveness. Revised and expanded edition. New York: Shocken Books.

14. My explanation of this phenomenon is that many Jews consider themselves, in many respects, as a nation as well as a community of believers.

Chapter Seven

Conclusion: Values in Psychotherapy

The concluding chapter returns to the underlying concepts of Judaic spiritual psychotherapy and expands upon previous writings and lectures delivered at academic conferences. It is divided into two parts addressing differing aspects of the topic. The first part deals with values in religion and psychology which, of course, is central to spiritually oriented psychotherapy. The second part examines, on a deeper level, the role humans and psychologists who deal with emotional well-being play. It ties that role into the overall design of the Almighty for creation. It, therefore, seems desirable to divide the chapter into two semi-autonomous sections.

PART I

We are confronted with a knotty problem. Is it possible to envision a valueless religion or, conversely, can a psychology embedded in a value system be considered scientific? Guttman writes,[1] "There are religions in which ethics occupies a position of eminence—as for instance in Judaism, where ethics constitutes a determining and decisive principle—while there are religions that lay greater stress on other values. However, there is no religion—or almost no religion—where ethics does not constitute a religious postulate."

As to psychology, including personality and clinical psychology, can it justify its claim to objectivity; can it be considered an empirical science if it is connected to a value system?

I will attempt to show that, contrary to the above suppositions, it cannot be assumed that values (primarily moral and ethical values) and religion are intrinsically and inextricably linked, or that psychology and values are not. The paths followed by theologians, philosophers, and psychologists relevant to this issue will be traced, and it will be demonstrated how this has led to a convergence, to a measure of common ground, by scholars of both disciplines.

Defining religion is not a simple or easy task. Tylor[2] defined religion "as a belief in spiritual beings." Paul Tillich[3] speaks of religion as "that which concerns us ultimately." In a similar vein, but in great detail Bellah[4] states that "religion is a set of symbolic forms and acts which relate man to the ultimate condition of his existence." The above do not, of course, exhaust the list of definitions of the religious process. These have been chosen because of what seems are their contrasting views as to the role and place of values in their conceptualization of religion. Tylor's definition does not mention values, whereas Tillich's, by calling attention to "ultimate concerns," seems to include them. There are those who may argue that concern with the ultimate does not necessarily include ethics and morality. The opposing positions have been documented and analyzed by the philosopher Bartley.[5] Insofar as Tillich is concerned, there is no question that his definition is meant to include them. This position is consonant with that of the existentialist psychotherapist Rollo May.[6] His description of religion refers to the feeling that life has meaning precisely because it is affirmed through creative living stressing purpose and values. On the other hand, Whitehead's[7] declaration that religion is "what the individual does with his own solitariness" seems to exclude ethical and moral values.

The American psychoanalyst Mortimer Ostow[8] offers an incisive analysis of the place of morality in the general scheme of religion: "It is the fact that religion can demand adherence to a code of behavior that makes it possible for religion to recommend and urge morality. Morality is not an intrinsic element of religion (except for the two central prohibitions of incest and murder), but as I mentioned above, was introduced into western religion by means of the spiritual monotheism of Biblical Judaism . . . In essence, a morally irrelevant act could have as much religious value, that is value in reducing ego pain by seeming to be a transaction with the father God as a moral act. To incorporate moral behavior into religious observance was an act of genius which made religion an institution which not only relieved some of the psychic pain of daily life, but also made it a powerful force for social order and cohesiveness."

The above is a clear instance that pristine religion is not to be equated with morality. Ostow views the confluence, the merger, between the two as an expression of genius and Judaism's unique contribution to the conceptualization of religion as the theoretical underpinnings of moral behavior. This, according to Ostow, is possible because religion can demand adherence to a code of behavior. It remained for Judaism to link this code of behavior to ethical moral behavior.

Ostow's belief that religion is associated with a code of behavior is not universally accepted. Randall[9] is of the opinion that, while some religions, such as Judaism, Islam, as well as the major eastern religions stress behavior or conduct, Christianity, in sharp contrast, had come to mean primarily a faith to be believed in, correct orthodox beliefs about God and man and human destiny. The differing emphases as to the comparative importance of behavior vis-a-vis faith in the structure and composition of religion illustrate the point that moral behavior, indeed behavior in general, is not essentially an integral part of religion, but rather an outgrowth of historical developments. It seems appropriate at this point to comment on Randall's conception of Judaism as a law to be followed, rather than a faith in which to believe. It seems more accurate to describe Judaism as an integrated interlocking system of beliefs and conduct. His conception of Judaism lays the groundwork for its being criticized as legalistic, a critique ably repudiated by the American theologian Niebuhr.[10]

The casting together of religion and morality has not encountered universal approbation. In his book *Psychoanalysis and Religion*, Erich Fromm[11] heatedly criticizes the tendency of both the religious and non-religious to view them as indivisible. His critique is based upon his understanding of the difference between ancient Egyptian religion and Greek culture. He believes the former to be a prototype of religion in which the priest is the physician of the soul, in contrast to Greece where that function was assumed by the philosopher. He chides the modern world for having abandoned the Greek ideal. He develops the thesis that psychoanalysis can assume the mantle once worn by the Greek philosophers. This, he believes, will benefit mankind by freeing it from the mistaken assumption that living a moral life means living a religious life. He writes, "I have tried to show in this chapter that the psychoanalytic care of the soul aims at helping the patient to achieve an attitude which can be called religious in the humanistic though not in the authoritarian sense of the word. It seeks to enable him to gain the faculty to see the truth, to love, to become free and responsible, and to be sensitive to the voice of his conscience. But am I not, the reader may ask, describing an attitude which is more rightly called ethical than religious? Am I not leaving out the very element which distinguishes the religious from the ethical realm? I believe that the difference between the religious and the ethical is to a large extent only an epistemological one, although not entirely so."

Fromm sees his thesis, expounding a moral code not based in religion, as rooted and embodying the Greek and Renaissance tradition. However, he neglects the changes wrought in the conception of religion due to the philosophical questions raised by Hume and addressed by Kant. These questions are related to the problem of the role of knowledge in western religion, which is a major issue in intellectual history. Indeed, this is the title of Randall's book, *The Role of Knowledge in Western Religion*. He feels that three main positions have been held in the west as to the place of knowledge and truth in the religious life. He describes the second position thusly: "Secondly, it has been held that Christianity is indeed a revelation of the truth, but this special knowledge is unlike all other knowledge in that it deals with a 'higher realm,' a realm inaccessible to rational inquiry and its methods; or with a quite different aspect of experience from other knowledge . . . Since the time of Kant its proper object has often been held to be the 'realm of values' with which scientific methods cannot deal, as over against the 'realm of fact' which science has appropriate techniques for testing. Since the rise of concern with a 'religious experience' conceived as something quite unique with a distinctive object of its own, 'religious' knowledge has been held 'to be knowledge of the special and peculiar object of this experience—that which the mystic's vision beholds, the 'Holy' or the 'Numinous,' 'Existential Truth'" (p. 8).

It is not Randall's intention to maintain that religion's preoccupation with morality is a modern phenomenon, but rather that since Kant, religion in certain circles has been identified solely with morality. This has evolved in order to create an impregnable fortress for religion, safe from scientific onslaught, from the constant changing of the understanding of truth. Viewed thusly, Fromm's critique of the state of affairs identifying religion with morality is misguided and inaccurate. He, of course, objects to institutionalized dogmatic religion, but in liberal Protestant circles religion has shed dogma and is identified with morality and ethics. Fromm seems to err on two counts: Firstly, his perception of religion as having always been identified with morality, an identification which he feels hinders progress is, according to both Ostow and Randall, incorrect, albeit for different reasons. Secondly, for many religionists, religion is primarily and almost solely definable as ethical, not dogmatic, a position which is so close to his that one wonders to what he is objecting and, therefore, what prompts him to cast psychoanalysis as the new religion designated as the guardian of values and the truly ethical life.

Another result of Kant's critiques was the turning by theologians to a reliance on "religious experience" as the crux and essence of religion. This was Schliermacher's aim, to free religion from its dependence on metaphysical beliefs. Proudfoot[12] evaluates Schliermacher's contribution as allowing religion to be appreciated as an autonomous moment which is not reducible to science, metaphysics, or morality. In sum, the response to Kant in religious circles was, as Randall noted, to: (1) identify the religious life solely as the moral life, incidentally a position severely criticized by Kierkegaard (Bartley[13]); or (2) free religion from its ties and dependence upon metaphysics and morality and root it in human experience. The latter tendency has been channeled into two directions: (a) Schliermacher's and others' insistence on the primacy of affect, on a sense of feeling and emotion; and (b) James', and to a greater extent, Otto's approach, emphasizing the cognitive aspects as basic to the religious experience (Allport,[14] Bertocci[15]). These have important consequences for understanding the philosophy of religion. The emphasis on subjectivity, the exclusion of the cognitive components by Schliermacher and others, and the concomitant neglect of norms due to the above emphases have been severely criticized by Soloveitchik[16] and Tillich.[17] Rabbi Soloveitchik[18] views with great apprehension the position which tends "to deliver philosophical thinking from the yoke of reason" and regards this as one of the causes of the unleashing of the dark forces of the 20th century. He writes, "When reason surrenders its supremacy to dark, equivocal emotions, no dam is able to stem the rising tide of the affective stream . . . Indeed, it is of greater urgency for religion to cultivate objectivity than perhaps for any other branch of human culture."

Not to do so is to nurture dark passion and animal impulses which can and have caused havoc and devastation. Rabbi Soloveitchik[19] is sympathetic to the concept of the direct religious experience, but anchors it to objectivity and norms—Halaka. (See notes 16,18)

He[20] elaborates on this theme in relation to prophecy which he distinguishes from mysticism precisely because it harbors a normative message. To this he adds a most interesting comment: were it not so, he reasons, prophecy would be secretive, egotistical, and therefore non-democratic. Law, norms, is the factor, the force which fashions the democratic character of the meeting between God and man. Following this line of thought, it can be argued that the inclusion of ethics and morality in religion is important not only for their intrinsic value, but because they embody normative behavior which is crucial to ensure the democratic nature of religion. No one is above the law and all are equal before the law. This concept translated and transposed to the theological sphere certifies the dignity of every man and woman before the Almighty. Tillich (See note 17) is strongly critical of the position, exemplified by what he terms the earlier Heidegger, of extreme subjectivity. As we have seen in Soloveitchik's writings, Tillich also points to the potential for destructiveness inherent in this approach.

Modern psychology has also grappled with the problem of the place of values—ethics and morality—in its framework. Psychology, as an empirical science, is a modern phenomenon and, therefore, took pains not to permit values to gain entry into its methodology. This position, it believed, would qualify it to be accepted in the rigorous scientific community. Clinical psychology is an even later development than most other branches of psychology, and is rooted in medicine as well as in psychology. As such, it was viewed by its practitioners as governed by the same principle operative in medicine, i.e., that the therapeutic relationship between patient and therapist is not to be influenced by the value systems of either one of them. This dual influence, the empirical legacy of science and the ethical impartiality of medicine, formed the prevailing attitude that moral values are not to be reckoned with in the therapeutic process. Hartmann,[21] one of the major figures in psychoanalysis, writes, "The only goal of the psychoanalytic method is to undo repressions and all other defenses against seeking unpleasant truth. It has nothing to do with ideologies, indoctrinations, religious dogmas or teaching a way of life or a system of values."

It is, however, questionable whether in reality this goal is achieved or even honored by many analysts. Perhaps this is so because psychoanalytic thinkers did not restrict their theorizing to the etiology of psychopathology. They came to regard their theories as all-inclusive and valid for explaining all of human conduct, normal as well as pathological, social as well as individual. Definite and specific ideas were held to be the truth concerning human nature; what originated as hypothetical came to be regarded as gospel truth. The usual reservations and healthy questioning, which is the hallmark of empirical science, were abandoned in a heady rush to embrace psychoanalytic explanations of all facets of culture. Needless to say, these conditions are not conducive to adopting a neutral stance when evaluating or relating to differing modes of behavior, including moral behavior.

Hartmann's position has been criticized on a number of points. Zilboorg[22] (cited in Higgins) writes, "Psychoanalysis . . . found itself able to go along officially without moral values not because it rejected these values but because it carried them implicitly and inherently as everything human carries them."

He is in effect saying that psychoanalysis is a value system. Hartmann would probably maintain that he was not referring to what may be considered universal moral values, but to a specific moral system or systems stemming from a particular culture and unique lifestyle. In whatever fashion this issue may be resolved, it remains a fact that the humanistic school in psychology, the "third force," evolved because of what many considered psychoanalysis' neglect of values. We have seen an example of their thinking in Fromm's proposal to regard psychoanalysis as an exercise in values.

Singer[23] contends that the therapeutic process is based on more than a simple acceptance of moral and ethical principles. It seems to rest upon the proposition that human dignity is affirmed only if man/woman is allowed and able to freely choose among alternatives. A person who is enmeshed, embroiled, all wound up in his/her emotional entanglements is simply not free. Therapy is to be viewed as bestowing freedom, as releasing the patient from irrational restrictions, restoring him/her to the dignity befitting a human being.

Freedom of choice is also an essential component of the Judeo-Christian heritage. Judaism conceptualizes the meeting of God and man in terms of a covenant (Soloveitchik; see note 20) which was sealed by ritual entered into freely (Exodus, 24:3-9). The concept of free will is the foundation on which the principle of Divine retribution is based. Theologically it is invoked to explain the raison d'etre of creation. In his commentary (Exodus, 13-17), Nachmanides, the Ramban, unequivocally states that God created the world solely that mankind can come to realize, affirm, and testify to this. Rabbi M. H. Luzatto, in the second and third chapters of his *Derech Hashem*, elaborates on this theme. God's purpose can be realized only if man, in at least a small measure, can be like Him. This, he explains, means that the spirituality, the goodness that he/she achieves, is to come about as a result of struggle—it is not be handed on a silver platter. This would demean man/woman, transforming him/her to a robot-like state.

This analysis defines a common ground on which religion and therapeutic clinical psychology meet. A major purpose of religion is to free humanity from being bound and servile to materialism, rendering mankind fit to achieve spirituality. The goal of therapy is directed toward freeing man/woman from pathological defects. Both are concerned with freedom, itself definable as a value and, furthermore, one that forms the cornerstone of the ethical moral edifice. This shared area of religion and psychology, both acknowledging and accepting the realm of values, ethics, and morality as relevant and momentous to their fields is, however, a far cry from Fromm's attempt to view psychoanalytic therapy as a religious process. Others, such as Robinson,[24] have sought to tie psychoanalysis to religious roots. Bakan (cited in Havens[25]) has this to say concerning psychoanalysis: " . . . can be understood as a part of, and a contemporary fulfillment of, the style of religiosity that starts with Abraham."

It has been, I believe, amply demonstrated that, although there are similarities and points of convergence between religion and therapy, the above statement and other similar pronouncements are unwarranted and inaccurate.

Another point bears closer scrutiny. If the above arguments are well founded, then to what exactly did the humanistic school of psychology object? If, indeed, dynamic therapy, in contrast to behaviorism, for example, is predicated upon freedom and its goal is the fostering of a greater measure of choice by the individual, then what fault did they find in psychoanalytic dynamic therapy? It seems that their objection is to Freud's and others' perception of human nature and motivation. His theory is biologically rooted, believing that man's energy and will to act stem from biological needs and drives. To a large extent, these theoretical deficiencies were rectified by later generations of ego and object relations theorists. Nevertheless, distinctly human traits and characteristics, such as altruistic idealistic behavior, are accorded secondary attention in their theory of behavior. Esthetics, religion, etc., are considered mere offshoots of sublimatory workings of the dynamic process. To this they object; for them, Freud's conception of human nature is wanting, sterile, and nonsensical.

General academic psychology has also shed its provinciality and deems it legitimate to study phenomena once considered as not being able to be studied scientifically. One of the leading American psychologists expressed this as long ago as 1971. McClelland[26] said: "I believe that psychology must deal with substantive moral issues, with content. Academic psychology in America has sold out to process—to perceiving, thinking and adjusting, learning. It is odorless, colorless, and idea-less, concerned only with the how of process, not with what is perceived or learned . . . Views and values don't get into the research, not openly." "Clinical and humanistic psychologists are in revolt, as I am in revolt, against the lack of substance. Many are the sons of preachers and most of them became violently anti-religious. They formed a new religion out of psychology."

This rather harsh pronouncement graphically illustrates the emotions engendered by the issues raised.

PART II

This section analyzes the role played by humans who attempt to alleviate emotional distress. It perceives this undertaking as fitting into the design of the Almighty for the world.

The unity of God is the cardinal principle of Jewish theology. This was publicly proclaimed by the Patriarch Abraham and reached its zenith at Sinai. Its parameters were defined by Maimonides in his Thirteen Principles.

This unity is not self-evident. God's majesty and complete sovereignty are not concepts that are universally accepted. Aside from the fact that idolatry still flourishes, other features, such as the presence of evil, pose difficulties which seem to diminish His unity. A large segment of the Jewish prayer book—the Siddur—expresses our desire that His kingship be established and accepted by all of mankind. We pray that what strikes people as contradicting His majesty-unity be recognized as false and misleading. A prayer recited three times a day ends with the wish that He and His name be one. A name is a label by which something is known. Praying that His name be one means that He be acknowledged as one, that His unity will be accepted and plurality shunted aside.

How can this ideal be achieved? This requires addressing some basic issues. What is the purpose of creation? A corollary of this is why did creation carry in it imperfections, the ability to sin? The sages teach that God wishes to be accepted and crowned by beings who willingly and freely choose to do so.[27] The term, willingly, implies that this process if fraught with pitfalls. There can be instinctual temptations to act immorally, or faulty cognitive intellectual reasoning which leads man astray. By their actions, humans can either realize God's intention or cause what seems to be a diminishing of His majesty. This ability or power of man/woman is what defines his/her duality—good inclination vs. evil inclination. It influences our perception of the Almighty; He can be perceived as awesome and yet close, or as removed from us as if there are other powers that determine our fate, as "one" or as fragmented—a duality. Our perception of God's unity is dependent upon man's achieving unity. This relationship will be elaborated upon later. At this point, better understanding of this thesis calls for psychological analysis of human personality.

Psychological theories of personality are divided as to whether man/woman is a holistic being, that he/she has a basic core personality shaping all his/her thoughts and actions, or is a person essentially an actor functioning according to what the situation dictates.[28] Social psychologists favor the second position, whereas a host of other theorists, dynamic and trait theorists, hold to the first. There are important theoretical implications as to which approach is favored. For example: (a) Do humans have a core self that we can identify as the real Martin or Diana? (b) Is there a unique component to each individual? (c) Can he or she be relied upon to act consistently? Sociologists and social psychologists quote Shakespeare's line in *As You Like It*: "All the world's a stage, and all the men and women are merely players."[29] If so, humans are not necessarily consistent from one situation to another, or over a period of time. Freud, however, believed that a person's core personality is formed during childhood. William James proposed that by age 30, a person's tendencies are set like plaster, never to change.[30]

Let us consider an important consequence of this debate. Assuming that a person has an inner core or self, or that each person has a unique configuration of traits, the question arises as to whether this entity is basically good, evil, or neutral. Staub sees Rogers and Maslow as believing that man is basically good. Freud believed that man/woman is basically selfish. The views of Konrad Lorenz, who has had a profound influence on psychologists, are akin to those of Freud. Rollo May, the existential psychologist, debated Rogers on this point. This issue is related to yet another question as to whether human aggression is innate, inborn. Some theorists and researchers feel that it is, and yet, "much evidence supports the contention . . . that for humankind, innate patterns of behavior are infinitely modifiable and flexible.[31]

We now turn to a description of human personality from the Judaic point of view. Genesis 2:7 teaches that the body was created from the earth, infused with a soul and became a living creature. Whereas there are no conceptual difficulties regarding the body, the soul—being of divine origin—is a complex entity having a number of components. The Kabbalah lists three: chaya, yechida, neshama. The term, neshama, also denotes the entity comprising the above three parts. The fusion of body and soul is problematic from a theological point of view. What is the nature of this fusion? Does a new entity emerge? Drawing upon Kabbalistic sources, the Gra identifies this entity as the repository of feelings and senses, the being which eventually will stand in judgment and be rewarded or punished—the ruach, which can be translated as the spirit. The ruach is the part of the person having and exercising freedom of choice to do good or evil. It is the uniquely human component of the person. It is distinct from the soul—neshama—which is divine in the sense that it can be considered a segment of the Creator.[32] The Gra's disciple, Rabbi Hayim of Volozhin, elaborated upon this concept of personality. He writes that the body, the material self, is inclined to sin. A person can, however, choose to lead a just and holy life and thereby transmute the body into a spiritual entity. He states that evil and the power it wields were created so that humans, the pinnacle of creation, can subjugate them, causing them to disintegrate. This is the purpose of Creation, to acknowledge God's majesty and unity. Rabbi Hayim sees this evil force as active only in our materialistic world. It is not of any consequence, does not exert any influence, in a sense does not exist in other spiritual worlds.[33] This concept does not leave room for rebellion by Satan, by evil, as envisioned by John Milton in his epic poem *Paradise Lost*.

The portrait of human character that emerges is as follows. The I—the ruach-spirit—is perceived as subjected to opposing pressures. Basically, the person is good due to the enveloping embrace of the divine neshama. However, the world has to be structured in a way that ensures complete freedom to choose between good and evil. This means empowering the evil inclination as well as creating external conditions conducive to sin, emphasizing the materialistic, non-spiritual aspects of life.

Rabbi Shneur Zalman, the founder of Chabad Chasidus, states in the first chapter of his classic work, *Tanya*, that there are two souls—neshamot—one divine, the other rooted in the non-spiritual component of humans. In Chapter 29, he deduces from the prayer recited every morning, "the soul—neshama—that you have implanted in me is pure": that the neshama is not the "I," the person. The person is the receptacle, the recipient of the divine neshama. His concept of the structure of personality, the duality of the person, is very similar to that described above.

We are now better prepared to understand on a deeper level how man's efforts, his/her striving toward unity, toward subjugating evil, lead toward the greater glorification of God's majesty. Here, we look to the Ramchal-Luzatto to instruct us. He does so in a number of his works, the most important of which, as regards our topic, is *Da'at Tevunot*. We cannot, of course, cover this in depth; we will just note a few of his central ideas.

The most basic principle that defines and governs the nature of the relationship between the Almighty and humans is one which the Ramchal explains rather briefly in this work. Rabbi Hayim of Volozhin places it as the cornerstone of his approach. It is axiomatic that God is perfect, that His essence, His majesty, does not require anything of us. Our good or evil doings do not add to or detract one iota from His essence. Rabbi Hayim quotes the verses (Job, 35:6,7)—free translation): "If you have sinned, you have not harmed Him . . . if you have performed good deeds, you have not given Him anything." He is above our praise; moreover, His essence is unknowable. How, then, are we to understand prayer? What is the nature of our relationship with Him? A relationship is possible and indeed demanded of us, because God chose to relate to the world and reveal Himself to mankind. The nature and extent of this contact are fully dependent upon us. When we supplicate Him to become close to us, to listen and hopefully grant our requests, we are asking that His bonding with us, with the universe, be closer and stronger—that He become more unified with the world He created. When we sin, He chooses to become distant. As regards His bonding with the universe, we were selected, in essence, to become His partners. This is an awesome privilege and responsibility.[34]

This principle, the distinction made between His essence and His relationship with humans, is one that is relevant to another extremely important issue, one with which theologians and philosophers grapple. God is viewed as transcendent, above and beyond everything. On the other hand, the immanence of God, His presence in everything, which, or course, signifies His solicitude for us, is an article of faith. These are two seemingly contradictory beliefs. The principle presented is a fundamental key to understanding the Judaic solution to this quandary.

God chose to reveal Himself to humans. His reasons for choosing to do so and to bond with humans are summarized by Luzatto-Ramchal, as follows: The simplest explanation is that God's traits (as perceived by us) are that He is merciful, kind, forgiving, etc. These traits are evident only in His relations with created beings. Secondly, His goodness dictates that others benefit from these traits. To fully appreciate the goodness bestowed upon him/her, the recipient must be in a position to feel that this was earned; it is not charity, not a dole. This necessitates creating a world in which acting properly, morally, entails overcoming temptation. On a deeper level, the reason for His revelation is that the Almighty wishes to be acknowledged as such.[35] We cannot fathom this fully, because, as noted before, His perfection is absolute and is not dependent upon our actions; nevertheless, He so wishes. The evolution of this process if manifested in all that transpires. All history, including the evil components, furthers this end. The mechanics of this process—how and in what ways God reveals Himself, what role evil has in the process of the unfolding, the revealing of God's majesty—is the subject matter of *Da'at Tevunot!*

The process can be viewed as evolving from apparent duality—our present perception of Him—to unity. The seeming duality will eventually be shown to be a misrepresentation, a faulty understanding of history. To fully understand the interrelationship between our actions and the Almighty's relation to us, we return to the debate as to who man/woman is—whether there is a central core or whether people react to situational circumstances. Man has a neshama—soul—which, by definition, is a segment of Divinity and is whole, not fragmented. However, human behavior is not always governed by the neshama—soul. The soul will very often fail to influence the "I," the ruach-spirit. In such instances, the "I" acts or reacts to the situational components which may be in opposition to goodness. This is man's duality. If man/woman achieves unity, if his "I" follows the advice of the divine neshama—the divine soul—he, in turn, shapes and influences God's relation to the world. God then manifests Himself, reveals Himself, in all His splendor. The hymn *Adon Olam* expresses this lyrically:

> The master of the universe who reigned before any form was created. At the time when His will brought all into being—then as "king" was His name proclaimed. After all has ceased to be, He, the awesome one, will reign alone . . . He is one—there is no second–

other.

NOTES

1. Guttmann, Y. I. (1976). On the Philosophy of Religion. Jerusalem: The Magnes Press. PP. 31-32.
2. Tylor, E. B. (1924). Primitive Culture, 7th ed. New York: Brentanans Press.
3. Tillich, P. (1951). Systematic Theology, Vol. 1. Chicago: University of Chicago Press.
4. Bellah, R. (1964). Religious evaluation. American Sociological Review, Vol. 29.
5. Bartley, W. W. III (1971). Morality and Religion. London: Macmillan, PP. 52-56.
6. May, R. R. (1940). The Springs of Creative Living: A Study of Human Nature and God. New York: Abington-Cokesbary. P. 91.
7. Whitehead, A. N. (1926). Religion in the Making. New York: Macmillan. P. 58.
8. Ostow, M. (1959). Religion. In American Handbook of Psychiatry, Vol. II. Ed. S. Arieti. New York: Basic Books.
9. Randall, J. H., Jr. (1958). The Role of Knowledge in Western Religion. Boston: Starr King Press.

10. Niebuhr, H. R. (1963). The Responsible Self. New York/London: Harper & Row. PP. 168-169.

11. Fromm, E. (1950). Psychoanalysis and Religion. New Haven, CT: Yale University Press.

12. Proudfoot, W. (1985). Religious Experience. Berkeley: University of California Press.

13. Bartley, Note #5, PP. 38-39.

14. Allport, G. W. (1950). The Individual and His Religion. New York: Macmillan.

15. Bertocci, P. A. (1971). Research on Religious Development: A Comprehensive Handbook. Ed. M. P. Strommen. New York: Hawthorn Books.

16. Soloveitchik, J. B. (1983). Halakhic Man. Philadelphia: Jewish Publication Society of America. (Notes to part 1, #4).

17. Tillich, P. (1951). Systematic Theology, Vol. 1. Chicago: University of Chicago Press.

18. Soloveitchik, J. B. (1986). The Halakhic Mind. New York: The Free Press, Macmillan. Pp. 53-58.

19. Soloveitchik, J. B. (1979). Ubikashtem Meshom. In Ish Halakah—Golu Venistar. Jersualem: Histadrut Ziyonit Olamit. (Hebrew)

20. Soloveitchik, J. B. (1965). The Lonely Man of Faith. Tradition, Spring. Publication of the Rabbinical Council of America.

21. Hartmann, H. (1960). Psychoanalysis and Moral Values. New York: International Universities Press.

22. Higgins, J. W. (1959). Contributions from related fields. In American Handbook of Psychiatry, Vol. II. Ed. S. Arieti. New York: Basic Books.

23. Singer, E. (1965). Key Concepts in Psychotherapy. New York: Random House, P. 128.

24. Robinson, L. H. (1986). Psychoanalysis and religion: A comparison. In Psychiatry and Religion: Overlapping Concerns. Ed. L. H. Robinson. Washington, DC: American Psychiatric Press.

25. Havens, J. (Ed.). (1968). Psychology and Religion: A Contemporary Dialogue. Princeton, NJ: Van Nostrand.

26. McClelland, D. C. (1971). Psychology Today, Vol. 4, #8.

27. Luzatto, M. C. (Ramchal), Gra, quoted in "Emuna and Hashgacha," Shmuel of Slutzk (Jersualem, 1999 second publishing) P. 20. See also Nachmanides (Ramban) commentary on Torah, Exodus (Parshat Bo). 13:16.

28. Hall, C. S., and Lindzey, G. (1957). Theories of Personality. New York: John Wiley, PP. 19-27. Baron, R. A., and Byrne, D. (1987). Social Psychology, 5th ed. Boston: Allyn & Bacon, Chapter 14. Myers, D. (1998). Psychology, 5th ed. Worth Publishers, Chapter 14.

29. Quoted by Kovacs, M. Who Am I? Torah and Psychological Definitions of Self (B'Or Ha'Torah, Vol. 15. 5765/2005) P. 82.

30. See Social Psychology, note #2. P. 494.

31. Aronson et al., quoted by Rabinowitz, Judaism and Psychology: Meeting Points. Northvale, NJ: Jason Aronson, 1999, PP. 21-22.

32. See note #5, Judaism and Psychology, P. 35.
33. Judaism and Psychology, PP. 36-37.
34. Hayim, Rabbi of Volozhin. Nefesh Hahayim (printed many times since first published in the 19th century). Especially important for our discussion is Gate #2.
35. Luzatto, Rabbi Moshe Hayim. Daat Tevunot. Edited and annotated by Hayim Friedlander, Bnai Brak, 1977. PP. 21-22.

www.ingramcontent.com/pod-product-compliance
Lightning Source LLC
Chambersburg PA
CBHW031555300426
44111CB00006BA/322